D1106312

From the foothills to the bay,
It shall ring,
As we sing,
It shall ring and float away;
Hail, Stanford hail!
Hail, Stanford hail!

From the Stanford Hymn

Stanford
From the Foothills to the Bay

Peter C. Allen

STANFORD ALUMNI ASSOCIATION & STANFORD HISTORICAL SOCIETY

Stanford, California

Acknowledgments

Editor-in-Chief:
Della van Heyst

Managing Editor:
Debby Fife

Art Director:
James Stockton

Photographers:
Peter Henricks
Leo Holub

Associate Editor:
Kay Daley

Researcher:
Susan Riggs

Staff Assistant:
Mark Bauer

Production Assistant:
Lawrence Peterson

Contributors:
Editorial/Donald T. Carlson, Ralph P.
Davidson, Timothy Enos, Thomas M. Newell,
Clark Sterling
Photography/Bill Apton, Robert Beyers,
Charles Comfort, Charles Painter, Tom Tracy

Library of Congress Catalog Card Number
80-50763

ISBN 0-916318-02-8

First Edition
Printed in Japan

Stanford: From the Foothills to the Bay is an under-taking that has required the assistance of so many people that, regretfully, we can extend to most of them only a general thank-you. Among them were more than 50 deans, directors, information officers, and others who gave their time to interviews with the author, digging up information, or reading the manuscript.

To the following we extend special thanks:

Richard W. Lyman, president of the University, Robert M. Rosenzweig, vice-president for public affairs, and William E. Stone, director of the Stanford Alumni Association, for their support throughout.

James T. Watkins IV, founding president of the Stanford Historical Society, who first proposed the book, Harvey Hall, president of the Stanford Historical Society, and Bowen H. McCoy and Mary Carroll Wineberg Scott, successive presidents of the Stanford Alumni Association.

Kenneth C. Christensen, chairman of the special Alumni Association and Historical Society advisory committee, and the committee members: Richard M. Blois, Donald T. Carlson, Marriner C. Eccles Jr., David C. Fulton, Melvin B. Lane, Norman B. Livermore, Carolyn McKnight, and Gunther Nagel.

Roxanne Nilan, University archivist, and her staff—Barbara Begley, Mary Blessing, Margaret Coesfeld, Mary Lawrence, and Mary Leopold—for being unfailingly helpful.

Mrs. Leland W. King, researcher into the history of the Stanford Museum, and Gunther W. Nagel, long-time student of Stanford lore, whose writings and advice were especially useful.

Bridget C. Morgan of the Facilities Office staff for furnishing architectural data.

Raymond F. Bacchetti, vice-provost for budget and planning, for a timely endorsement.

All of us engaged in producing *Stanford: From the Foothills to the Bay* found the assignment to be demanding, but—like the University itself—one that rewarded us with education and a great deal of pleasure.

P.C.A.
May 1980

Leland Stanford Jr. on his pony
Palo. Alto. May 1879
photographed. May 1879
by Eadweard Muybridge
1
17 18 19 20 21 22 23 24 25 26
A series of 8 phases of a stride by
a pony while cantering. Photographed
on wet collodion plate.
E.M.

Table of Contents

The California Wonder OCCIDENT, owned by Gov. L. Stanford.
Time in harness, a private trial of speed.
2:19   2:19   2:19.

Introduction

Stanford University and William James got to know each other well during the academic year 1905-06. The philosopher of the learned brothers James—then 64, a dean among scholars and perhaps the most influential thinker of his day—was serving as a visiting professor to fulfill a request made by Jane Stanford shortly before her death.

When Stanford president David Starr Jordan asked him to deliver the annual Founders' Day address on March 9, 1906, James took as his topic "Stanford's Ideal Destiny." Since the University was then a mere 15 years old and still not free of financial problems created by the death of Senator Stanford, the high optimism expressed by James made for heady listening.

"Leland and Jane Stanford," James said, ". . . saw the opportunity for an absolutely unique creation; they seized upon it with the boldness of great minds."

The site? "Classic . . . in its atmosphere of opalescent fire, as if the hills that close us in were bathed in ether, milk, and sunshine."

The climate? "So friendly . . . that every morning wakes one fresh for new amounts of work."

The architecture: "Noble."

Life was democratic and sharing, he continued, traditions were original. Then, warming to his theme, he called the quality of academic work "astonishingly good, both in the faculty and in the student body."

Stanford, he averred, "only needs a boldness like that shown by her founders to become the seat of a glowing intellectual life sure to be admired and envied the world over. Let her claim her place; let her espouse her destiny."

Now Stanford is entering the tenth decade of its first century. Its site remains one of rare

and uncrowded beauty, if not always as opalescent as before. The noble Quads survive, life is still democratic. Most important, Stanford has responded to James's call to greatness. It has transformed itself from a small and insecure institution a continent away from the nation's cultural summit into a world-class university, "the seat of a glowing intellectual life." And, as the lives of universities are measured, Stanford is still a youngster.

The Palo Alto Farm

Creation of the San Francisco Peninsula was a rather recent event in geologic time. It happened some half a million years ago when melting glacial ice raised the level of the Pacific Ocean. Seawater, probing a defile at the Golden Gate, flooded southeasterly into the lowland, leaving a mountainous thumb of land that fell away to broad terraces and marshes along the inner curve of a shallow bay.

Indians, extending their long migration southward from Alaska, found the shores of the bay hospitable. Several thousand years ago the Ohlone tribe established a comfortable hunter-gatherer civilization along the Peninsula and as far south as Big Sur.

The first recorded sighting of San Francisco Bay by Europeans was made by a party foraging for the Gaspar de Portola expedition of 1769. Back in camp, wrote Portola's diarist, the hunters reported that from high ground of the Peninsula "they had seen an immense arm of the sea or *estero,* which extended inland toward the southeast as far as the eye could reach; that they had seen a beautiful plain adorned with a variety of trees; and that the columns of smoke that they had observed all over the level country showed that there were many *rancherias* of Indians." These were the smokes of the Ohlone villages.

The Portola party worked its way down the Peninsula and camped on the bank of San Francisquito Creek, whose course marks a boundary of the Stanford campus. Whether they camped directly under El Palo Alto, the sentinel redwood tree that still stands at the edge of the creek just off El Camino Real, is not known for sure. The first to write a surviving record of the tree was Padre Francisco Palou, diarist of the de Anza expedition, who came five years later: "There is . . . a very large redwood which can be seen for more than a league before reaching the arroyo, and from a distance looks like a tower."

El Palo Alto—literally "the high stick"—became a trusted landmark as Spanish boots and cartwheels carved out the California mission trail, and it served as a corner marker in the early 1800s when Mexican land grants created the adjoining Rancho Rinconada del Arroyo de San Francisquito and Rancho San Francisquito. (El Palo Alto is the centerpiece of the seal of Stanford University.)

In 1876 Leland Stanford purchased a 650-acre section of Rancho San Francisquito for a country home. The Stanfords already had a palatial home 30 miles north in San Francisco—a huge Victorian castle into which Stanford had poured some of his profits from the Central Pacific. But they wanted an outdoor life for their eight-year-old son, Leland Jr., an only child born in the parents' eighteenth year of marriage. Stanford named his new property the Palo Alto Farm, and the elaborate horse-breeding operation that he installed there

Peter Coutts, the "Mysterious Frenchman," poured money into a showplace ranch next to the Palo Alto Farm, then suddenly sold it to Senator Stanford in 1881 and disappeared. Rumors abounded until it was learned years later that Coutts had been in temporary political exile from France because of differences with Napoleon III.

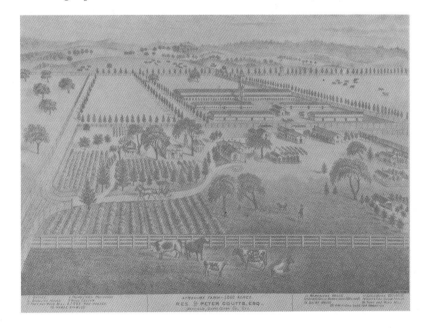

A storm tore away one of El Palo Alto's trunks in 1887.

was known as the Palo Alto Stock Farm. (Later, after Stanford University was opened in 1891, the town that sprang up across the Southern Pacific tracks was also named Palo Alto.) Stanford kept on buying adjoining properties until he owned more than 8,000 acres of flat and rolling land that extended from El Camino Real, the old Spanish trail, well into the foothills of the Santa Cruz Range.

The original purchase included a rather modest house adjacent to San Francisquito Creek near Menlo Park, and in time the Stanfords cut it in two and inserted a manorial three-story addition between the parts. The principal rooms were floored with quartered

Left: Governor's Avenue led from the house to the stock farm.

The Stanfords' home on the Palo Alto Farm. Leland Jr. kept a bicycle, a boat, guns, and riding horses at the country place.

oak planks, bordered with cherry wood. The library and first-floor hall were paneled in Honduran mahogany and the dining room in cherry. A skylight was rigged so as to ventilate the three-story main stairwell. But not all the planning was given to elegance. The contractor's specifications stated: "There is to be a place for a dog to sleep under the rear piazza, and the piazza is to be built around the pine tree which is in the way."

Stanford planted many trees around the house, including a row of chestnuts from seeds obtained from his boyhood home in New York State. His brother Thomas, who had migrated to Australia, sent him eucalyptus varieties, and it is probable that some of these

The gold spike, now in the Stanford Museum, shows the dents of the sledge hammer wielded by Leland Stanford at Promontory Point.

Above: Senator Stanford produced and sold wines from the Palo Alto Farm and other Northern California ranches. Right: Leland and Jane Stanford posed for Bonnat in Paris in 1884.

THE FOUNDERS

Leland Stanford, one of five brothers who made fortunes not as miners but as merchants in the California goldfields, was born on March 9, 1824, in Watervliet Township, New York. His father was a farmer, woodcutter, and sometime innkeeper along the Albany-Schenectady Turnpike.

Chosen as the son who would follow a professional career, Leland was admitted to the practice of law in 1848 and set up his office in Port Washington, Wisconsin. He and Jane Eliza Lathrop, born August 25, 1828, into the family of a successful Albany merchant, were married in 1850. Two years later, after a fire destroyed Stanford's law office and library, the young couple decided to join Leland's brothers in California. Leland went on ahead and roughed it for three years as a Stanford Brothers storekeeper in Mother Lode mining camps, sleeping on counters with his boots for a pillow. When he took over the main store in Sacramento in 1855, he brought Jane out from Albany.

Leland was a leader in organizing the Republican Party in California. Against slavery, he stumped the state for Lincoln in 1860 and then met with the new president in the White House. The following year, at age 37, he was elected governor and was deemed responsible for keeping California in the Union, although there were many Southern sympathizers in the state.

Early in the sixties Stanford joined with three other Sacramento merchants—Charles Crocker, Mark Hopkins, and Collis P. Huntington—in the building of the Central Pacific, the western link of the first transcontinental railroad. When the sale of stock failed—"[it] could scarcely have been sold by the bushel for ten cents," Stanford said—the partners personally went deeply into debt and drove themselves nearly to the breaking point as construction crews pushed the rails over the snowbound Sierra and across 600 miles of desert sand. On May 10, 1869, engines of the Central Pacific and the westward-building Union Pacific drew together at Promontory Point, Utah. Stanford, president of the Central Pacific Railroad Company, drove a gold spike to join the two rail lines and the blows activated a telegraph key that clattered across the nation: "Done!"

The university that Leland and Jane Stanford built in their son's memory at their Palo Alto Farm on the San Francisco Peninsula was opened in 1891. Leland Stanford, in the midst of his second term as a United States senator, died at Palo Alto on June 21, 1893. His wife, a wise and strong-willed woman who had been a full partner in planning the University, overcame great financial hardships in keeping it open until her husband's estate could be settled, and thereafter she directed the expansion of the campus. She died on February 28, 1905, in Honolulu.

Palo Alto Spring—1878 *shows the Leland Stanford family, relatives, and friends on the lawn at the Palo Alto Farm. Mrs. Stanford is dressed in white. Leland Jr. is in striped stockings, and the artist, Thomas Hill, has painted himself looking over the Senator's shoulder. Originally hung in the ballroom of the Stanford mansion in San Francisco, the painting is now in the Stanford Museum.*

were used to line the mile-long macadamized lane, now known as Governor's Avenue, that led from the residence to the trotting farm. It was a road the Governor (a title his friends continued to use long after Stanford's term as California's chief executive ended in 1863) took every chance he could get. The ex-farm-boy turned multimillionaire railbird loved to watch his trotters in training on the running track that was rolled and sprinkled each day at dawn. He would inspect the white-paled paddocks where he kept 30 stallions and 300 brood mares or take a turn around the nine large barns, the stables, the carriage house, and the grist mill. "I have seen the principal stock farms of America," wrote one visitor,

"and it is easy to say that no two or three of them rolled into one would duplicate Palo Alto." The blood lines Stanford chose and the training methods he devised were ridiculed by the trotting fraternity, but not for long: 19 world records were set under the Palo Alto colors between 1880 and 1895.

Leland Jr.—not at all the poor little rich boy—was a competent horseman and marksman. He spent hours riding through the woods and fields of the family estate, his dogs running at heel. He was interested in mechanics, and while on a European trip with his parents he wrote to a friend at home, "Mama and Papa have promised to give me a complete machine shop at Palo Alto." He helped lay

Leland Jr. liked to sketch trains, boats, bridges, and engines. This is from an 1883 notebook.

Above: A spur track of the elaborate railroad Leland Jr. built on the grounds of the Palo Alto estate. Right: A posthumous portrait of the son of the founders, one of several they had painted from a favorite photograph.

the track for his small-gauge railroad that wound among the gravel paths and lemon trees between the house and the stable, with spurs to the greenhouse and the creek. A hand engine and car were fashioned in the Central Pacific's Sacramento shops, for which young Leland wrote a gracious letter of thanks to the superintendent.

Young Leland, for all his love of the out-doors and machinery, was also a precocious student of languages and history. His parents encouraged these interests by taking him on trips to Europe, where they sought also to improve their health at Bad Kissingen or in the pure air of the Swiss Alps. Leland Jr. began collecting antiquities on these trips—first arms and trophies of war, later Greek vases, Egyptian bronzes, and other items of historical and ethnological significance. A room in the San Francisco mansion became his museum where he catalogued and dis-played his collections.

The family, accompanied by Leland's tutor, Herbert C. Nash, spent Christmas of 1883 in Vienna. After being snowbound for a week in Bucharest, they crossed the Danube, part of the way in sleighs over the ice to a small island, the rest of the way in open boats, then proceeded by train and boat to Constanti-nople. In Athens, where he persisted in his collecting though the weather was foul, Leland complained of a headache and sore throat. From Naples he wrote to a friend: "Mama and myself are not well just for the present because we have been going it too hard." In search of an easier climate, the family pushed on to Florence, but Leland's fever developed into typhoid and on March 13, 1884, two months short of his sixteenth birthday, he died. Because Palo Alto Farm was the best loved of all the Stanford resi-dences and the only one they always called "home," the parents brought Leland there. His body was placed in a temporary mausole-um erected in a grove of oak and magnolia trees near the house.

The Angel of Grief kneels in memory of Henry Lathrop, Mrs. Stanford's brother. It is located near the family mausoleum in the Arboretum.

Founding
and Planning

During Senator Stanford's first night of troubled sleep following the deathbed vigil in Florence, his son appeared to him in a dream and said: "Do not say that you have nothing to live for.... Live for humanity."

"How I wish I could remember all he said to me in that dream," Leland told Jane in a later recollection which she set down in her journal. "I know I resolved from that moment to build the University, and we both from that night resolved on this."

The death of their son brought to a focus the Stanfords' long-held plan for using part of their wealth for public benefaction. They had considered a museum, a hospital, a technical institute, but the idea of a university now appealed to them as the most suitable memorial to a son who had been just approaching college age. And they determined that this memorial should be located on the Palo Alto Farm, where Leland Jr. had spent an idyllic boyhood.

Governor and Mrs. Stanford had come from families of modest means and in the early years of their marriage had shared a life of hard work. So it was natural that their first thoughts were to establish an institution "where boys and girls can . . . grapple successfully with the practicalities of life." They did not wish to follow the ruling Greek and Latin tradition of higher education. But, as they conferred with the presidents of Harvard, Cornell, M.I.T., and Johns Hopkins, their thoughts matured into what was then the unusual concept of combining a cultural education with special preparation for personal success in the student's chosen profession.

This decided, Governor Stanford called for several good stenographers to come from San Francisco and, seated on the veranda at Palo Alto, he dictated without notes the

The monogrammed cover (right) and title page (below) from the copy of the founding grant that was signed by the trustees at their first meeting in 1885. Its elaborate calligraphy is spread over 40 sheets of parchment, 13½ by 16½ inches.

Frederick Law Olmsted, America's premier landscape architect, was consultant for the University's design. He told a friend, "There is not any word half big enough for [the founders'] ideas."

founding grant, providing for the endowment and defining in sweeping strokes the University's scope, responsibilities, and organization. Engrossed on 40 sheets of parchment by a noted San Francisco penman, the founding grant was presented to the 24 members of the first Board of Trustees, who formally accepted the duties outlined for them. At this simple ceremony on November 14, 1885, in the library of the Stanfords' San Francisco home, The Leland Stanford Junior University was founded.

In May of 1885 Leland Stanford had been elected to the United States Senate and, following the formality of the University's founding, he and Mrs. Stanford journeyed to Washington to set up yet another lavish household. The summer of 1886 found them back at the Palo Alto Farm to begin in earnest

the physical planning of the campus. In August they were joined by two distinguished consultants—Frederick Law Olmsted, America's foremost landscape architect and the designer of Central Park in New York, and Francis A. Walker, president of Massachusetts Institute of Technology.

Senator Stanford asked his coachman to hitch a strong team to a sturdy carriage and the three men set off in search of the best site on the 8,000-acre farm for the University buildings. It was the time of summer when foxtails and clover burrs clung to trouser legs and the spice of the white-flowered tar weed hung in the air. At one point the coachman opened a place in the fence and drove to a tableland atop a knoll. Spread before them were the dun-colored fields, green swatches of oak and chaparral, the blue waters of San Francisco Bay, and, beyond, the softly folded contours of the Diablo Range. It was a vista of compelling beauty. Here, said Olmsted, was the ideal location. But, after some discussion, Senator Stanford instructed his driver to take them to a gently sloping alfalfa field below. There they drove a stake which marked the southeast corner of the first group of Stanford buildings. The university he and Mrs. Stanford had in mind, the Senator explained, was going to need unlimited level space in which to expand.

This disagreement over the site was the first of several between owner and planner. Yet their prickly collaboration brought forth in the University's original quadrangles an architectural masterwork. "Both Olmsted and Stanford were powerful and brilliant men, not used to compromise," comments Paul V. Turner, Stanford University art historian. "Despite the difficulties of their collaboration, the design they jointly produced for

Olmsted's "Plan of Central Premises— 1888" shows for the first time Palm Drive and the Oval.

Stanford University was as powerful and brilliant as they."

After several weeks at Palo Alto, Olmsted and Walker returned to Boston and sent separate reports to the Stanfords. Olmsted quickly disposed of any thought of reproducing in California the typical Atlantic Coast college architecture based on Oxford and Cambridge models. "If we are to look for types of buildings and arrangements suitable to the climate of California, it will rather be in those founded by the wiser men of Syria, Greece, Italy, and Spain," he cautioned.

Walker wrote, "I would strongly recommend one-story buildings of stone.... Mr. Olmsted and I are fully agreed that, with proper architectural treatment, buildings of this character, made of massive rough stone, connected by an arcade, may be made singularly effective and picturesque upon the plain of Menlo." So the essential elements of the University's architectural distinction emerged from that long midsummer planning session.

Before the end of 1886 the planners were joined by the architect, Charles Allerton Coolidge, then 28 years old and at the beginning of a distinguished career. He and two partners had formed Shepley, Rutan & Coolidge as successor to the practice of their late mentor, Henry Hobson Richardson of Boston. Richardson had been widely acclaimed for his revival of Romanesque architecture. It was a style admirably suited to the Palo Alto environment and Coolidge applied it with vigor and imagination. There was one notable and felicitous innovation—apparently inspired by the California missions and suggested by Senator Stanford—and that was the system of interconnecting arcades supported by rhythmic progressions of arches.

Olmsted's master plan called for an inner

Jane and Leland Stanford laid the cornerstone of Stanford University on May 14, 1887, the nineteenth anniversary of their son's birth. It was, wrote a contemporary, "the beginning and seal of the visible university to which their lives and fortune were consecrated."

quadrangle of 12 one-story buildings and Memorial Church, facing onto a huge central courtyard and surrounded by an outer quadrangle of single- and multistory buildings. It was decided that only the Inner Quad buildings, except for the church, would be erected at the outset, and Coolidge came to Palo Alto in April of 1887 with a set of preliminary plans. Olmsted had reserved a site for the church on the western side of the quadrangle so that the north-south vista, as one approached up the stately main drive, would carry through the buildings to the foothills. The Stanfords, determined to achieve the formality and monumentality they desired in this memorial to their son and acknowledging that "a landscape architect and an architect might be disappointed," turned the quadrangle 90 degrees so that the front entrance was grander and the vista terminated at Memorial Church.

The Stanfords also surprised the architect by insisting that the cornerstone be laid

almost immediately, on May 14, the anniversary of Leland Jr.'s birth. Coolidge knew better than to tell Mr. Stanford that he should wait another six months for working plans. "What I did," he recalled years later, "was to order a spade and a brass band immediately."

Three hundred community residents and special guests assembled for the ceremony. It was a hot day and men and teams already at work leveling the site were raising clouds of dust. Casks of water and lemonade were placed under trees. Apparently Coolidge meant the brass band as a figure of speech, for the only music was provided by the choir of the Menlo Park Presbyterian Church. After the speeches, Senator Stanford troweled in the mortar and Mrs. Stanford, silently weeping, placed a corsage on the stone. The sandstone block and its bronze plaque, inscribed simply "The Leland Stanford Junior University, May 14, 1887," was built into a corner of the first Inner Quad building west of Memorial Church.

THE FAMILY MAUSOLEUM

The Stanford family mausoleum stands in the Arboretum on a site first selected by the Stanfords for a new Palo Alto country home. These plans were abandoned when Leland Jr. died in 1884 and construction of the University took precedence.

The granite and marble vault was built for the ages. The architect's specifications for the 25-by-40-foot structure called for excavating the foundations at least eight feet deep—"should good hard bottom not be found at this depth, continue deeper"—and for laying a two-foot-thick concrete base. The superstructure is of the best Barre, Vermont, granite, "free from iron or any imperfections"; the polished columns are of one stone each; and the roof consists of three huge slabs, each 26 feet long.

The interior is lined completely with highly polished Italian marble from Carrara, eight inches thick and secured with bronze anchors.

The three marble sarcophagi, hollowed to contain the caskets, are 8 feet 6 inches long, 4 feet wide, and 5 feet 6 inches high. They are decorated with floral wreaths of bisque and sterling silver.

The tomb was completed in 1889, five years after Leland Jr.'s death, but Mrs. Stanford preferred to leave her son's body in the temporary mausoleum which had been erected among the oak and magnolia trees near the family home. Senator Stanford's body was placed in the new mausoleum when he died in 1893 and the boy's casket was moved there early one morning soon thereafter, quietly and without ceremony. Mrs. Stanford and a companion visited the mausoleum nearly every day. They would arrange fresh flowers and sit inside for a while. The chairs of Roman design that they used are now in the chancel of Memorial Church.

When Mrs. Stanford died in 1905 more than 6,000 people came to the funeral, overflowing Memorial Church into the Inner Quad. They formed a processional four abreast down Palm Drive to the mausoleum.

Though only a stone's throw from busy El Camino Real, the mausoleum's setting is quiet and pleasantly bucolic, a place of whispering grass and giant trees, squirrels and quail. A huge live oak, whose limbs, spreading a full 60 feet, overarch the front walk, was saved by the attention of a man with whom Senator Stanford had frequently clashed. In a telegram from his Boston office, followed by a long letter, campus designer Frederick Law Olmsted gave his superintendent instructions for moving the tomb site several feet and for care in grading to protect the already impressive tree.

Stone Upon Stone

Mellow sandstone brought on flatcars from a quarry near San Jose was shaped into graceful arches. Capitals were carved with variations of scroll, leaf, block, and heart forms.

Construction of the University moved slowly. Quarrying and dressing of the sandstone blocks, the carving of capitals and arches, the laying of tile roofs—all were time-consuming processes. Coolidge and his draftsmen, set up in a small building on the site, were preparing the working plans a jump ahead of the builders. With Senator Stanford in Washington and Olmsted in Boston, decisions had to be thrashed out by letter. In 1888 Stanford's doctors ordered him to Europe, but the University was never far from his thoughts. While descending from the high Alps—muffled in furs and their carriage heated by hot stones—the Stanfords were approaching Lake Silva Plana when the Senator caught sight of a hotel that matched his idea of a dormitory for men. A quick letter to Coolidge, enclosing a pencil sketch of the hotel, became the basis for Encina Hall.

Roble Hall, the residence for women, was barely ready in time for the opening of the University, which finally had been set for October 1, 1891. By June work still had not started on Roble, although the cut blocks of sandstone had already been delivered to the site. When it appeared that the enrollment of women might be delayed for a year, Mrs. Stanford insisted that the much faster Ransome process of concrete construction be used. She was familiar with the process, which produced a rough, stone-like surface, because it was being used in another project she was hurrying to completion—the Leland Stanford Junior Museum along the Oval in front of the Quad. The dormitory was finished with a few days to spare and a young man who was taking progress photos of the construction came upon Mrs. Stanford on a ladder hanging curtains in a second-story room. (The name, Roble Hall, was transferred to a new building in 1918.)

Meanwhile, David Starr Jordan, the progressive young president of Indiana University, had been appointed Stanford University's first president. Named late in March of 1891, he had precious little time in which to find professors, form a curriculum, and recruit students—all by October 1. Luckily, he was a man of action. "Dr. Jordan caught fire instantly, like a pitch-pine kindling," a colleague observed. "He appointed a professor the very day he accepted his own position." But he quickly found that established scholars in the East were not willing to rough it out West. "In the Back Bay," Jordan commented, "are men whom nothing would induce to go west of Springfield." Drawing on his experience at Indiana, Jordan turned to younger scholars who showed promise. No one in the first group was older than Jordan, then 40, and most were nearer 30.

Senator Stanford had set the size of the first

A serious-miened faculty posed on the steps of Encina Hall during the second semester of the first year.

faculty at 15, and Jordan, stretching the number a little by not counting the registrar, the librarian, and the foreman of the woodworking shop, had completed his roster by the first of June. When 465 students showed up on opening day, instead of the expected 250, Dr. Jordan scrambled to increase the teaching staff and the *Register* for the second year listed 49 assistant, associate, and full professors. The "Old Guard," as these early appointees came to be known, for the most part vindicated Dr. Jordan's judgment. They stood by him and Mrs. Stanford through the hardships that followed Senator Stanford's death, and a significant number served until retirement—terms of 30 years or more. Many

became eminent in their fields. They set standards for themselves and for the selection of their colleagues that have carried forward to this day.

The Jordan family arrived at the Menlo Park train station toward the end of June. "I carried in my arms our little boy, being at the same time further emburdened with hand luggage," the new president remembered. "This modest arrival commended me highly to 'Steve' Gage, one of Senator Stanford's cronies, who was waiting with him at the station, curious to see what manner of man I might be. When asked later for his first impression of the new functionary, Gage replied: 'I guess he'll stand hitched.'"

The Inner Quad took shape slowly over a four-year period as workmen winched the heavy rough-hewn blocks and striated columns into place. The Quad's beauty comes from simple, massive forms and the color and texture of the materials.

The prexy batted clean-up in the annual senior-faculty game.

DAVID STARR JORDAN
First President (1891-1913)

David Starr Jordan once said, "When the evidence seems to be in, I like to say yes or no at once and take my chances." So did he react when Senator and Mrs. Stanford offered him the presidency of their university in March of 1891; he accepted the same day. The 40-year-old Jordan was then president of Indiana University and already, having been a favorite protégé of Agassiz, was recognized as an outstanding ichthyologist. He was later to add a third demanding activity, that of a leading apos-tle of world peace. One reason Jordan could follow three callings at once was his exceptional memory. Whenever a new lot of fishes from some distant place had been spread out on tables in the Stanford zoology laboratory, the president would be given a call. He would stride up and down like an officer reviewing troops, and, unerringly, he would stop before a species new to science. "Ho," he would exclaim in his great sonorous voice, "that's a new face!" Jordan lived out his last years in Serra House at the end of an oak-shaded campus lane. When he died in 1931, he had spent half of his 80 years at Stanford.

Orrin Leslie Elliott, destined to be registrar of the University for 34 years, had traveled West with the Jordans. The day after their arrival, though 300 workmen still swarmed over the site, the two men set up for business in the first Inner Quad building just west of Memorial Court.

Jordan, a large and friendly man, was a gifted educator, scientist, and humanist. He also had a poet's way with words. To him the California poppies in the Stanford meadows were "great orange cups which drink in the sunlight but close with the shadow." The irregular series of ridges that rise behind the campus he called "a misty camp of mountains pitched tumultuously," and, looking across San Francisco Bay to the Sierra del Monte Diablo, he saw a "summer cloak of ripened wild oats, overwashed at sunset by translucent amethystine hues." At the University's opening day exercises, he said, "These long corridors with their stately pillars, these circles of waving palms, will have their part in the student's training as surely as the chemical laboratory or the seminary room. Each stone of the quadrangle shall teach its lesson."

That opening day in the autumn of 1891 was bright and sunny. The great arch at the western end of the Quadrangle had been backed with panels of light and dark cloth to form an alcove where the dignitaries sat. "To right and left of the platform," wrote Ellen Coit Elliott, wife of the registrar, "pampas plumes and palms sprang fifteen feet up into the light. Below them palmettos and the delicate sprays of the bamboo encircled the rostrum's edge and were themselves encircled by long festoons of grapevine, with grapes in gigantic clusters drooping heavily. Overhead fluttered bright banners. Within the alcove fell the rich folds of the Stars and Stripes,

and from its background the portrait of the boy Leland Stanford looked down upon the scene with serious eyes."

When Senator Stanford moved to the lectern, Mrs. Stanford stood at his side, her arm linked in his, her parasol held to shade him from the sun.

"In the few remarks I am about to make," the Senator began, "I speak for Mrs. Stanford, as well as for myself, for she has been my active and sympathetic coadjutor and is co-grantor with me in the endowment and establishment of this University.... This ceremony marks an epoch in our lives, for we see in part the realization of the hopes and efforts of years; for you, faculty and students, the work begins now."

Right: David Starr Jordan speaking at the dedication of the University on October 1, 1891. Senator and Mrs. Stanford are seated in the front row. About 2,000 chairs had been set up on the Inner Quad and they were filled to overflowing. Riding horses, carriages, and farm wagons were hitched to every fence and at half past ten a special train from San Francisco pulled up on the spur track that was used during construction.

Overleaf: The Inner Quad in 1891. The 12 original buildings enclose a huge courtyard (250 by 600 feet). Today towering trees rise from the eight planting islands.

A soft breeze barely stirred the trees when Senator Stanford's funeral was held in the open air of the Inner Quad. The pallbearers, eight senior locomotive engineers on the Central Pacific, placed the coffin in the hearse and the procession to the family mausoleum in the Arboretum began.

There were many difficulties at first. More professors had to be recruited, faculty housing was woefully inadequate, microscopes and books were late in arriving from the East. Even the class bells were not operating and the passing periods were signaled in true Western fashion by the jangling music of a triangle that hung in one of the archways. But there was something in the air that brought forth the strong sense of "family" that has been a distinguishing trait of the University ever since. Part of it must have been the unity that comes from sharing vicissitude. Part of it must have been the friendliness—the professors were scarcely older than the students and even Dr. Jordan would greet passersby with a sweep of his soft, wide-brimmed fedora. Part of it must have been the warming embrace of the sandstone Quad and of the acres of grass and trees that sheltered the campus. And part of

it certainly must have been the exhilaration of breaking new academic ground, freed from the dead hand of rigid classicism. "Hope was in every heart," recalled one of the original professors, "and the presiding spirit of freedom prompted us to dare greatly." Before long Dr. Jordan had adopted as his motto for the University a phrase from the militant sixteenth-century German poet Ulrich von Hutten— "Die Luft der Freiheit Weht," which is usually translated "The Winds of Freedom Blow."

Leland and Jane Stanford attended the 1893 commencement in the men's gymnasium. The Senator had to be steadied up the steps of the platform by men at each side. He was to have spoken but did not. A few days later, early in the morning of June 21, 1893, he died in his sleep at the Palo Alto home at the age of 69.

Top: Escondité Cottage (left) on the Coutts ranch, where the Jordans first lived, still stands. The former Hoover home (right) is now the home of the University president. Middle: Ten frame houses appeared on Alvarado Row in the summer of 1891. Below: The Hanna-Honeycomb House.

THE FACULTY SETTLES IN

Today there are more than 600 single-family faculty homes and 82 condominium apartments on campus land. When the University was about to open in 1891 there were none, and the nearby towns of Mayfield and Menlo Park provided only rundown hotels and houses that one faculty wife said would be called shanties back East.

During the summer of 1891 ten cottages were hastily built along Alvarado Row. They were, recalled Ellen Coit Elliott, "the same size, the same distance apart, and all toed the mark alike." But soon grass, trees, marigolds, and trumpet vines softened the effect. Blue-bloused Chinese brought fruits and vegetables along the back lane in heavy baskets slung from poles across their shoulders. The piped-in water was coffee colored so drinking and cooking water had to be drawn in buckets from an artesian well across the street.

Other faculty homes quickly spread out along Alvarado, onto adjoining streets, and finally up the gentle slopes of San Juan Hill. Near the crest of the hill Mr. and Mrs. Herbert Hoover built in 1919 a spacious home that was to be their permanent base, though Mr. Hoover's activities took him to many parts of the world for extended periods. After Mrs. Hoover's death the house was given to the University in 1944, and, named Lou Henry Hoover House, it is now the residence of the University president.

Another famous campus home is the Hanna-Honeycomb House, designed by Frank Lloyd Wright. When Wright took the commission from Professor and Mrs. Paul R. Hanna in 1935 he set out to "break open the box" of conventional rectilinear buildings. The redwood home, which merges into rising ground off Frenchman's Road, is designed entirely in hexagonal shapes. It has been designated by the American Institute of Architects as one of 17 buildings among the more than 400 designed by Wright that should be preserved as examples of his architectural contribution to American culture. The Hannas gave the house to the University in 1977 as the residence of a distinguished visiting professor.

As the faculty increased rapidly in the fifties and sixties and housing became tight in the surrounding communities, additional campus land was opened to leasing for faculty homes on Pine Hill and Frenchman's Hill. Demand was so great that lot choices were determined by drawings. The homes of faculty and senior staff now occupy approximately 500 acres.

Times of Adversity

Senator and Mrs. Stanford had reserved to themselves control of the University's affairs during their lifetimes, including the parceling out of "all the money that could be wisely used." Mrs. Stanford had remained in her husband's shadow—on opening day she could not bring herself to deliver the short speech she had written out. But following the death of the Senator she, at age 65, took on full responsibility for the University with unsuspected strength.

While the estate was being settled—and this was delayed by an unsuccessful government suit demanding early payment of railroad bonds, which went all the way to the Supreme Court—there was barely enough money for the University to scrape by. Several of Mrs. Stanford's advisers urged her to close the campus down, at least temporarily. "Stop the circus," was the callous demand of Collis P. Huntington, a Central Pacific partner who had had a bitter personal falling-out with Stanford. But Mrs. Stanford and Dr. Jordan, with the faculty's cooperation, managed to keep the doors open and maintain high academic standards. When the estate was released from probate in 1898 after what Dr. Jordan termed "six pretty long years," the president expected to restore faculty pay cuts and move quickly to the expanded academic program he had envisaged for so long. Mrs.

The Richardson-Romanesque style is prominent in the pre-earthquake Memorial Church. Mosaic angels of faith, hope, charity, and love are tucked into the curves of the church's archways.

Stanford had other thoughts. She wanted to see constructed during her lifetime the rest of the buildings that she and her husband had so often talked about.

Mrs. Stanford turned first to the buildings of the Outer Quad, contracts for two of which had been on Senator Stanford's desk for signature at the time of his death. Coolidge, before his departure in 1893, had designed the eight multistory and six single-story buildings and the ponderous Memorial Arch at the main entrance, and his plans were generally followed, although modifications were made by local architects. Construction of these buildings stretched from 1898 to 1906; the last, Geology Corner, was finished but not occupied just before the 1906 earthquake struck. When the Outer Quad was safely under way, Mrs. Stanford turned to four other major buildings—Memorial Church, for which Inner Quad space had been reserved from the outset, the Chemistry Building, a new library, and a new gymnasium.

Mrs. Stanford was described as being "devoutly thankful" when she felt at last she could use funds to build the church which she and her husband had decided would be the central structure of the University, signifying their deep religious feelings. Walking late one afternoon through the Inner Quad with John Casper Branner, the University's vice-president, she told him, "While my whole heart is in the University, my soul is in that church." Memorial Church, she decided, would be its name, for it was to be erected in memory of Senator Stanford.

Again a design by Coolidge was available, showing inspiration from Richardson's plan for Trinity Church in Boston, and modifications were made by Clinton Day, San Francisco architect. Mrs. Stanford watched closely the smallest details of construction. Charles E.

Mrs. Stanford in 1897, four years after her husband's death. She had guided the University through financial crises and was soon to begin the massive construction program she and Senator Stanford had planned.

The powerhouse smoke-stack was immortalized in an old Stanford drinking song: "Oh, I wish I had an ocean of rum, of sugar a million pound, /The dear old Quad to mix it in, the chimney to stir it round. . . ." Will Irwin, Class of '99, was the author.

Hodges, resident architect, recalled that she would follow him along the high scaffolding, holding onto his coattails. "She inevitably carried a parasol," he said. "It was notched at the lower end. She would run it into the carving and if it did not come up to the mark, she would ask me to have it cut a little deeper." The notch indicated how far the same parasol had penetrated medieval carvings in Europe. In Florence she ordered statues of the Apostles for the chancel and, in order to select the marble, she and Bertha Berner, her long-time secretary and companion, traveled to the Carrara quarries in an open car pulled on wooden rails by a little engine.

In Venice she arranged with A. Salviati and Company to design and install the extensive mosaic work on the interior and exterior of the church. The 19 principal stained-glass windows were executed by F. and J. Lamb, Tenafly, New Jersey. All are adaptations of familiar religious paintings except for one, an original by the Salviati designer, showing a child being borne to heaven by angels. The child bears an unmis-

takable resemblance to Leland Jr. Ranged around the interior walls are 28 inscriptions of inspiring messages, attributed to no one. They came from a notebook in which Mrs. Stanford jotted down quotations that appealed to her but that she later would paraphrase to suit herself. Memorial Church was dedicated on January 25, 1903, although two more years were to pass before the mosaic work was completed.

Dr. Jordan came to call this period of unceasing construction "the stone age." Mrs. Stanford disliked the phrase and sent the president a letter of gentle rebuke in September of 1904. Dr. Jordan replied promptly: "I am in the fullest sympathy with the plan of putting up the buildings first and . . . I have been very patient (for me) with the necessary limitations in this period of building. But it is my duty to look after the weak places in the University and I know and our older students know that the professors are working under great difficulties."

But Mrs. Stanford's sense of duty to the intentions of her husband was unshakable. Within months she was ready to break ground for a large library and a gymnasium, located across the Oval from the museum and the Chemistry Building, which had been completed in 1903. These latest buildings, departing completely from the Quads, were in Classical styles. A second-story room in the library was to be an exact replica of the library in the San Francisco mansion—even the furniture would be moved—and was to serve as a meeting room for the Board of Trustees.

Wearied by nearly 12 years of devotion to University affairs and troubled by a household accident—a trace of cleaning fluid had somehow gotten into her bedside bottle of Poland water—Mrs. Stanford sailed for

Honolulu on the steamer *Korea* in February of 1905. She died there, apparently of a heart attack, on February 28 at the age of 76. After funeral services in Memorial Church, students conveyed the casket to the family mausoleum.

As the years have passed there has been a tendency to think of Mrs. Stanford as a meddling woman who valued only limited aspects of the University rather than seeing it as a whole. It would be well to renew the appeal of President Branner in his Founders' Day address of 1917 to forever keep alive "the ennobling ideals and aspirations of the woman who was the real founder and the greatest benefactor of Stanford University."

The day before leaving for Hawaii Mrs. Stanford had written an address for the laying of the cornerstone of the library, but she asked that the ceremony be delayed until spring when the condition of the grounds would be better. Expecting to be in Honolulu, she selected a student, Alex Sheriffs, class of '06, to read her address and this he did at the ceremony on May 15. While agreeing that "we need books at present more than anything else," Mrs. Stanford had written: "My fondest wish has been to live long enough to give to you young students all the requisite buildings planned by the founders. . . . The 'stone age,' which has been so frequently alluded to, no doubt was irritating and tedious to some connected with the University, but to me the erection of these stone buildings has had a deep and important significance."

A young Stanford student, Carl Breer, Class of '09, perched atop the dome of the nearly completed library to snap this picture of the campus basking in the sunlight—perhaps its last portrait before the great earthquake struck.

The entrance gates on Palm Drive at El Camino Real settled into neat piles of rubble.

A year later—at 13 minutes past 5 a.m., April 18, 1906—the earth beneath Stanford's handsome new buildings shook violently for more than a minute. The campus community poured into the streets. "By dozens, they crowded out to peer into the whirling cloud of dust which concealed the Quadrangle," wrote Edith R. Mirrielees, a senior English major and later professor of English at Stanford. "From the engineering block, masses of steam rose volcano wise; from the fallen church and arch quantities of fine, bluish dust mingled with steam, giving to the whole an appalling appearance of present danger, but hiding, for a moment, the extent of the injury. As the dust settled, ruin after ruin stood out in sharp relief against the blue of the morning sky."

Two persons were killed—a student who was in the path of an Encina Hall chimney that broke through four stories to the basement, and a fireman who was caught in the fall of the great stone smokestack of the powerhouse behind the Quad.

The damage to buildings, while appalling, was not as great as first suspected. The tower and flying buttresses of Memorial Church fell, wrecking the chancel and literally blowing out the front wall, reducing the magnificent mosaic of the upper facade to rubble. The nearly finished library and gymnasium, Memorial Arch, brick additions to the museum, and many of the arches supporting the Outer Quad arcades were completely wrecked. The walls of the four Outer Quad corner buildings and the Chemistry Building were damaged considerably, and there was lesser damage to several other structures.

Repairs were started by the end of June

Below, left: The 1906 earthquake brought the massive steeple— clocks, chimes, and all— crashing into the interior of Memorial Church. The concussion destroyed the mosaic facade. Below, right: Columns of the arches between Memorial Court and the Inner Quad were shoved out of line.

Death in 1905 spared Mrs. Stanford the sight of devastation to her beloved University. Right: The ponderous Memorial Arch and the church tower were beyond saving. Below, left: The new library never held a book; the broken stalk of the 100-foot chimney of the powerhouse is a monument to the night foreman who was killed by its falling stones. Below, right: The Stanford family home.

Student spirits were only momentarily dimmed. Many students, as did this group in front of Encina Hall (left), camped out for several days before being sent home. The Chi Psi house (right) was pitched nearly intact off of its six-foot foundation. Below, left: The numbered stones of Memorial Church await reassembly around a new steel skeleton.

and, despite a two-week labor strike, enough of the buildings were ready to allow resumption of classes at the start of fall quarter.

"The Memorial Church, splendidly built but wrecked by the fall of its spire and flying buttresses, touches us deeply...," Dr. Jordan wrote to his friend, Andrew White, president of Cornell. "But the new library, gymnasium and Museum annex, crushed like a pie set on edge, we have no feeling for." Eventually plans for restoring these unloved structures, as well as the ponderous Memorial Arch, were abandoned. Memorial Church was taken down stone by stone and completely rebuilt— except for the tower—with a strengthening steel skeleton. The organ and stained-glass windows, miraculously unhurt in the quake, were reinstalled and the Salviati artisans returned from Venice with new sets of mosaics. The church—reopened in 1913 and completed in 1916—accounted for about half of the $1,200,000 reconstruction cost.

44

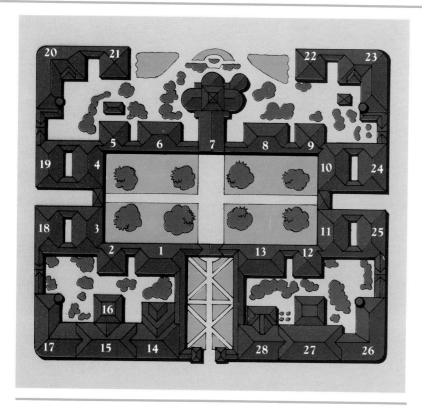

FAITH AND LEADERSHIP

The architectural statement of Memorial Church—as a structure and in its religious symbolism—is so powerful it tends to obscure the fact that the church, like any community church, is a place of worship and of sacred music. It is also a center of volunteer service, fellowship, and education. "The primary objective of Memorial Church is a religious one, to bring students to a clear and tranquil faith in God," Dean of the Chapel Robert Hamerton-Kelly has stated. "We also have an educational objective, to train young people in the kind of leadership which would be applicable in any field. The latter objective is one we share with the University in general."

Map Key

(Uses listed are current uses. For former uses and other information, see Building Inventory, page 223. For map of entire campus, see pages 74-75.)

1. **Building 1.**
   Dean of Graduate Studies; Dean of Humanities and Sciences; Dean of Undergraduate Studies; Chicano Affairs.
2. **Building 10.**
   President; Vice-President and Provost.
3. **Building 20.**
   Classics.
4. **Building 30.**
   African and Afro-American Studies; Comparative Literature; Modern Thought and Literature.
5. **Building 40.**
   English.
6. **Building 50.**
   English.
7. **Stanford Memorial Church.**
8. **Building 60.**
   Humanities Special Programs.
9. **Building 70.**
   Religious Studies.
10. **Building 80.**
    Geology; Human Biology.
11. **Building 90.**
    Philosophy.
12. **Building 100.**
    Committee on Linguistics.
13. **Building 110.**
    Anthropology.
14. **Building 120.**
    Beginning 1982: Communication, Sociology.
15. **Building 160.**
    Political Science.
16. **Building 170.**
    Vice-President for Public Affairs; Academic Secretary; University Counsel.
17. **Building 200.**
    (History Corner formerly also English Corner); History; International Relations; Western Culture Program.
18. **Building 240.**
    German Studies.
19. **Building 250.**
    Asian Languages.
20. **Building 260.**
    (Engineering Corner) Spanish and Portuguese; French and Italian; Humanities and Sciences Administration; Slavic Languages; Ombudsman.
21. **Building 300.**
    Classroom; unassigned office space.
22. **Building 310.**
    Affirmative Action; Academic Planning.
23. **Building 320.**
    (Geology Corner) Geology.
24. **Building 360.**
    Biogeology.
25. **Building 370.**
    Values, Technology and Society Program.
26. **Building 380.**
    (Alfred P. Sloan Mathematics Corner; formerly Physics Corner) Mathematics.
27. **Building 420.**
    (Jordan Hall) Psychology.
28. **Building 460.**
    (Margaret Jacks Hall) Computer Science; Boys Town Center for the Study of Youth Development.

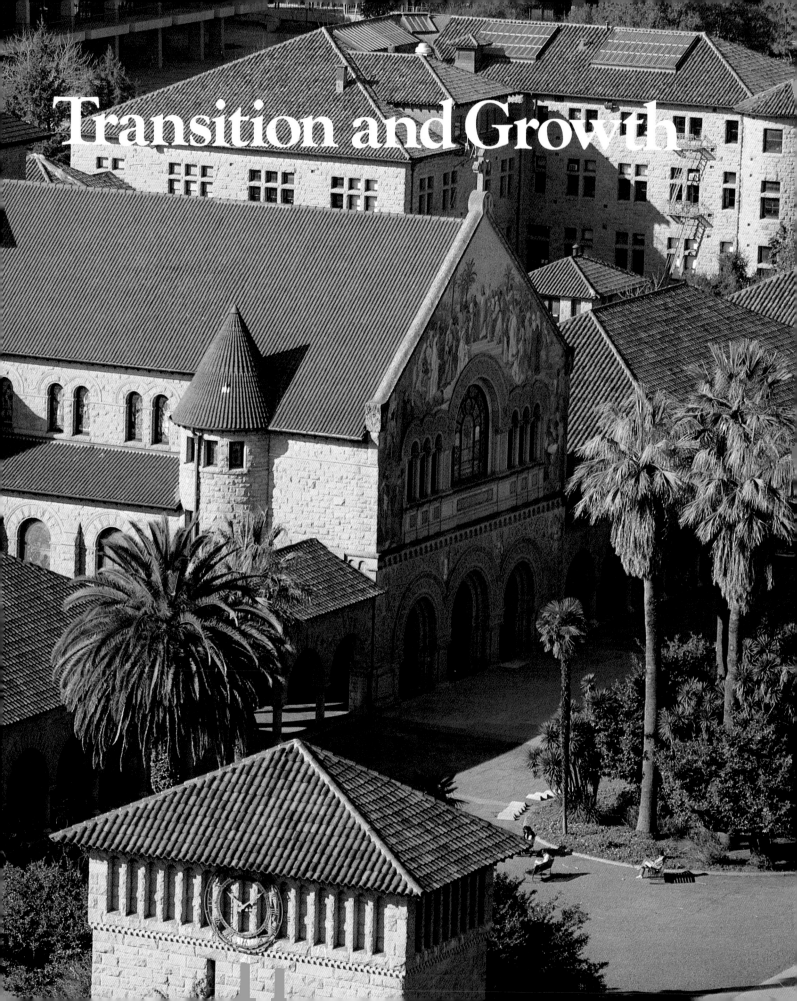

Transition and Growth

On the very day of the 1906 earthquake Dr. Jordan had received a letter offering him the position of secretary of the Smithsonian Institution. It was a job he had long desired, but he declined. "I am sure that my place is here," he wrote to a friend. "I can now, I believe, weld this institution together. I need some years to complete this. Then the institution will be beautiful, with a great library, adequate apparatus, a strong and well-paid faculty and a small but selected and effective body of students.... I shall stay with the poppies, the perfect sunshine and the shadow of the great temblor."

But another cause—even more compelling than the help he once thought he could give to young naturalists as leader of the Smithsonian—began gradually to take more of Jordan's time. The cause was world peace and beginning in 1909 he took a series of leaves of absence to devote himself to it in this country and abroad. In 1913 the Board of Trustees—at the instigation of a recently elected member, Herbert Hoover, class of '95—arranged for Dr. Jordan to assume the new post of chancellor so that he could devote himself to nonadministrative University func-

tions and the peace movement. Thus drew to a close the 22 years during which he set Stanford's course and guided it through some of its best and worst of times.

John Casper Branner, vice-president of Stanford and an eminent geologist who had been Jordan's first appointee to the faculty, moved up to the presidency. His short time in office—he had insisted as a condition of acceptance that he would retire in two years when he reached 65—was marked principally by his campaigns to get faculty salaries increased (successful) and to get rid of the Medical School (unsuccessful). More buildings were not what the University needed at the time, and only two were erected during his tenure—the Women's Clubhouse and the

The Old Union and the newer White Memorial Plaza today form the hub of student activity.

The three buildings edging the Old Union courtyard now house the offices of the dean of student affairs, admissions, financial aids, registrar, and other student services.

JOHN CASPER BRANNER
Second President (1913-1915)

John Casper Branner, Dr. Jordan's first appointee to the Stanford faculty, was appointed second president by the Board of Trustees in 1913. In his inaugural address he said nothing to disturb his reputation as a reserved, methodical man of science. He pointed out that he would be serving only two years, until his retirement at 65. "You are liable to find me a rather unemotional university president," he prophesied. But when the board re- quested the new president to find ways of reducing expenses by eliminating some departments and combining others, they found there was inner steel in this modest and quiet man. "If the scholars are to be chased away or replaced by cheap instructors, I don't want anything to do with the outfit," Branner wrote to one trustee. In the end the board rescinded its request and adopted the president's increased salary budget.

"The Farm" lingers on: Sheep trimmed lawns in 1912; hay was mowed near Encina in 1935.

Men's Clubhouse. (The clubhouses were joined in 1922 by the Stanford Union and the three buildings, converted to offices for student services, are now known as the Old Union.)

Ray Lyman Wilbur, alumnus and physician to the University before becoming dean of the School of Medicine in 1913, was inaugurated as Stanford's third president in January of 1916. Stanford was then a university in transition. The many internal crises of its first quarter century had had a cloistering effect. "Our aim must be to bring the University directly into the currents of vital life in the world about us," the new president said.

Stanford owes much of its architectural style to Moorish Spain. "Certainly there is no closer tie than to Granada's famous Alhambra, built chiefly in the fourteenth century," Harry Sanders Jr., for many years Stanford's director of planning, has pointed out.

Enrollment had topped 2,000 but only a few more than 300 were graduate students. Dr. Wilbur put Stanford firmly back on its course toward becoming a full-fledged university. He expanded graduate study and professional education, promoted faculty research and outside consulting, reorganized the independent departments into schools, and generally promoted high scholarship. He switched from the semester to the quarter system so that buildings would no longer be virtually idle during the summer, with the faculty dispersed to the High Sierra or the Monterey shore. The regular class schedule, on the other hand, he shortened to end at 4 p.m. to encourage

"each man and each woman to go out each day for some healthful exercise."

The limitation of the number of women students to 500—set by Mrs. Stanford in 1899 and later to become one of the University's thorniest problems—was lifted by the Board of Trustees in 1933. It was not that Jane Stanford had been opposed to women students. She was in fact pleased to entertain them in her home and she recognized that they carried off as many scholastic honors as the men, maybe more. "Besides," she observed, "the refining influence of girls is wonderful." But she had become fearful that the rapidly rising proportion of coeds might turn the University

Left: Dr. Wilbur with Chancellor Jordan at his inauguration as Stanford's third president. Below: Physiology major Ray Wilbur in his Encina room with his two roommates.

RAY LYMAN WILBUR Third President (1916-1943)

Ray Lyman Wilbur's appointment as third president "caused hardly a ripple of surprise; it had been expected by nearly all who had followed the matter," reported the 'Stanford Alumnus.'

He was to be president for 27 years and then chancellor until his death in 1949. During his six decades at Stanford, one characteristic stood out: Wilbur was a man who knew his own

mind. An incident at the time of his inauguration was illustrative. Although Wilbur's aversion to academic gowns was well known, the president of the Board of Trustees tried valiant-

ly to convince him to wear one for the ceremony. Wilbur would not budge. "To me it was my business, not a Trustee's," he wrote in his memoirs. "But it was more than that. I knew that if I

let this president of the Board decide this question for me he would try to decide other more important questions, not through action of the Board but by pressure on me."

into a women's college—not, she felt, an appropriate memorial to her son. So, while parents began entering their daughters on the waiting list at birth and the number of rejected applications created much ill will, the enrollment of men climbed steadily. In 1933, when the ratio had reached about five to one, the trustees looked to the provision of the founding grant which required them "to afford equal facilities and give equal advantages in the University to both sexes," and removed the restriction.

Although building activity during the Wilbur presidency was limited by the Great Depression and the onset of World War II, substantial progress was made, beginning with the completion of the Thomas Welton Stanford Art Gallery in 1917. The heightened emphasis on research was reflected in construction of buildings at the Hopkins Marine Station (1918) in Pacific Grove; the Daniel Guggenheim Aeronautical Laboratory (1919), where W.F. Durand perfected the design of the airplane propeller; the Ryan High Voltage Laboratory (1926), where, at the dedication, spectators were awed as 2,100,000-volt flashovers between electrodes were made to leap 20 feet through the air; and the Hoover Tower (1941), steadfastly dedicated to peace though the nation was on the brink of war.

Increasing enrollment led to four new dormitories—a new Roble Hall (1918) for women; Toyon and Branner (1923) for men; and Lagunita Court (1934) to accommodate additional women after the lifting of the 500 limit. Much-needed Quad space was released for other uses by completion of the Main Library (1919), Memorial Hall (1937), and the Education Building (1938). Frost Amphitheater, planted with saplings, was ready in time for the 1937 commencement.

A rapid expansion in athletic facilities was triggered by the resumption of American football in 1919 after a period in which rugby had replaced it as the major fall sport. The Stanford Stadium (1921) was formed by excavating 232,000 cubic yards of earth with scrapers drawn by 100 teams of horses and mules. The playing field was placed 30 feet below ground level and the excavated earth was piled up around it to form the bowl. The unusual and beautiful Sunken Diamond (1925) for baseball was constructed near the stadium in the huge borrow pit that remained after the excavation for a Stadium enlargement project. Encina Pavilion (1922) for basketball, so adequate when it was built, was woefully inadequate by the time it was replaced 47 years later. The golf course (1930) is still rated for championship play, and the Women's Gymnasium (1931) replaced an old wooden gym that, converted to other uses, was renamed Woodpecker Lodge for good reason.

Left: The Women's Gymnasium in 1899. Below: When Encina basketball pavilion was converted to office space, stained-glass windows showing Hank Luisetti (No. 7) and his teammates in action were inserted in place of the old ticket windows.

Overleaf: Man and beast combined to build the 60,000-seat Stanford Stadium in six months. It was ready for the Big Game of November 1921. Charles B. Wing, professor of structural engineering, was the designer.

The 50-year-old championship golf course winds its way through some of the campus's most picturesque acreage. Fifty-six thousand rounds—recreational and varsity competition—are played there in a year.

The Wilbur era saw the end of running the University solely on income from the original endowment. In the beginning the endowment had been adequate—indeed, for a while Stanford was the most heavily endowed institution in the country. But in 1919 the trustees, with a nudge from Hoover, faced up to the need for more income and imposed the first tuition—a modest $40 per quarter. Soon thereafter Dr. Wilbur began the first all-University effort to raise funds from alumni, foundations, and others. As was expected, returns were slow. Mrs. Stanford's insistence that there be no outside gifts had led to the impression that the University would always

be rich beyond need. This attitude needed to be changed. The organization that set the University firmly to the task of raising money was Stanford Associates, a volunteer group formed in 1934 by 250 alumni. The trustees appropriated $10,000 to finance the Associates' first annual fund appeal, after which Dr. Wilbur, an ardent fisherman, commented, "Well, you got your bait back." Since then the catch has increased considerably.

Dr. Wilbur reached retirement age in 1940 but the trustees prevailed upon him to stay on through the celebration of the University's 50th anniversary the following year. This was both a serious and a gala event, centering around an academic symposium and dedication of the Hoover Tower at commencement time and a series of cultural and social events beginning October 1, the University's actual birthday, including a faithful reenactment on the Inner Quad of the opening day ceremony of 1891. Just as the anniversary year ended America went to war and Wilbur was again asked to stay on. This he did until Donald Bertrand Tresidder took office in September 1943.

Dr. Tresidder, Stanford alumnus and head of the Yosemite Park and Curry Co., resigned as president of the Board of Trustees to accept the University presidency. It was like searching far and wide for treasure only to find it in your own garden, Dr. Wilbur remarked. But the treasure was to be lost in a tragically short time. Dr. Tresidder died on January 28, 1948, while in New York on University business.

Tresidder's task was one of keeping the University's standards high during the straitened circumstance of the war and postwar years. Not much in the way of permanent construction could be done because of shortages and priorities, but the new president took far-reaching action in the area of planning. In 1945 he established the University's first Planning Office and appointed Eldridge T. Spencer, a noted San Francisco architect, as its director.

The Planning Office, as its first order of business, made a study of space and found that the utilization of classrooms, laboratories, and dormitories could be substantially increased. This information saved the day when the discharged veterans began flooding back. Enrollment in the fall quarter of 1945 was 3,725. In the fall of 1946 the number jumped to 7,244 and a year later it was 8,213. Facilities were jammed all day and into the evening,

Three generations of bookstores: The first was on an unpaved path between the Quad and Encina; the second is now the Career Planning and Placement Center; the third, built in 1960, was greatly enlarged in 1978.

DONALD BERTRAND TRESIDDER
Fourth President (1943-1948)

Donald Bertrand Tresidder had the gift of making friends—not least of all with Stanford students. "Spontaneously and genuinely, we like this rugged, friendly man," read a 'Stanford Daily' editorial a few days after he took office as University president. He understood Stanford students because he had been one who had worked his way through (A.B. '19, M.D. '27). His undergraduate studies were interrupted in 1917 when he enlisted in the Army and became a pilot in a bombing squadron stationed in Texas. At the time of the armistice he penned a long letter to one of his premed professors, a letter that forecast the seriousness of mind that marked his adult years. "If you hear of any work in the department regardless of how menial," he wrote in closing, "I hope you will let me know about it. I am writing Dr. Slonaker to see if his rats still need a keeper. I am not sure just yet how I am going to manage things to the best advantage but I have observed that obstacles are usually overcome as we meet them."

the faculty pitched in to teach more and larger classes, and administrators scrambled to make ends meet. The University moved quickly to acquire Dibble General Hospital in Menlo Park from Army surplus; renamed Stanford Village, it provided 300 apartments for married students and 1,500 dormitory beds. Despite paper-thin partition walls, balky kerosene stoves in the kitchens, and other make-do arrangements, many Village alumni have happy memories of time spent there.

In 1947 Lewis Mumford, the prominent regional planner and social philosopher, came to Stanford as a planning consultant. His report strengthened a premise of the Planning Office that Inner and Outer Quads should be maintained as the functional core of the University. Praising the University's original conception as "the work of the most mature and effective mind America has so far produced in city planning and landscape design," Mumford stated: "A fresh, independent analysis of the problem brings one back to Olmsted's essential contribution: compactness, concentration, unity."

A start in this direction had been made with the reestablishment of the president's office on the Inner Quad, where a building was completely remodeled inside and, taking advantage of the 20-foot ceiling of the original, a second floor was inserted. The vacated Administration Building on the Outer Quad was remodeled into a multifloor home for the Law School.

Another of the Planning Office premises was that the University should provide adequate housing for the majority of its students. Shortly before Dr. Tresidder's death a contract was let for the first unit of Crothers Hall for law students and funds were received for Lucie Stern Hall for undergraduate men.

A SYLVAN RETREAT

The Laurence Frost Amphitheater, even when filled to its capacity of 12,000, can seem like a place apart, a space of its own. The steep sides of the sylvan bowl rise 50 feet—20 feet below ground level and 30 above—and are lined with varieties of oak, birch, California bay, sycamore, and spruce, their upper branches interlaced to form a mass of greenery. Interspersed, showing their colors in season, are Japanese plum, liquidambar, maple, silk oak, holly, and mountain laurel.

"We wished to create an amphitheater where large groups of trees would give an effect of a heavily forested area—a pleasant, naturalistic setting," said Leslie Kiler, the landscape architect. Kiler, a graduate of Stanford in graphic arts in 1924, had studied landscaping at Harvard and in Europe.

Almon E. Roth, '09, Stanford controller at the time, is credited with first suggesting the amphitheater when he saw excavated dirt from the Memorial Hall and Education Building construction projects piling up on the 20-acre plot the amphitheater now occupies. The idea became reality when Mr. and Mrs. Howard Frost donated the funds as a memorial to their son, John Laurence Frost, '35, who died in his senior year at Stanford.

Kiler guided the shaping of the dirt, some 93,000 cubic yards in all, including topsoil skimmed from campus road projects. Then he launched a search for specimen trees, some of which were boxed and brought as far as 500 miles. Two thousand pounds of grass seed were broadcast on the stage area and on the rising tiers of the seating area.

The first use of Frost Amphitheater was the 1937 commencement, and graduation continues to be the bowl's biggest event. Another traditional program that has taxed the bowl's capacity is the summer pops concert by the San Francisco Symphony, for many years conducted by the late Arthur Fiedler, as a benefit for the Children's Health Council, and rock concerts have drawn large crowds. But Frost Amphitheater serves another, completely different role. Almost any time, spring through fall from early morning until evening closes in, students use the amphitheater for rest, meditation, quiet studying, or picnicking. It's a good place to get away from it all.

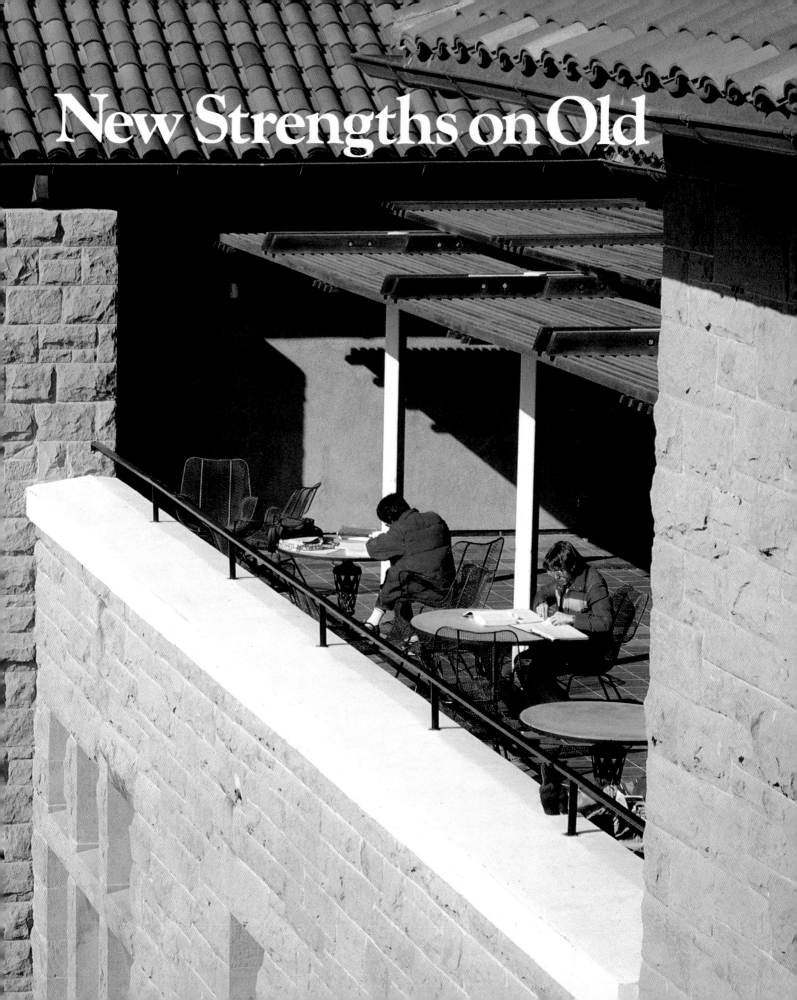

New Strengths on Old

Stanford's fifth president, J.E. Wallace Sterling, took office in 1949 on April 1 —and the humor of that being April Fool's Day was not lost on this physically large, personable, gifted leader.

The aftershocks of World War II were wearing off. The time had come—in Dr. Sterling's phrase—"to build new strengths on the old." The climate was propitious for higher education, and it was to remain that way through the fifties and early sixties. In 1974, on the 25th anniversary of his appointment, Dr. Sterling recalled:

"There was economic prosperity. There was public interest in higher education. A court decision opened the way for corporate philanthropy. There was the new and wealthy Ford Foundation. The Cold War, despite its tensions and tragedies, turned on the federal spigot in support of research. The first Eisenhower administration made available millions for health research facilities. And, while all this was going on, an ever-swelling number of Stanford alumni, Stanford Associates, and friends served faithfully and well to enhance the University's financial well-being."

During all of its pre-Sterling history Stanford had raised $31 million in gifts and bequests. During the 19 Sterling years the figure was $329 million. Enrollment, propelled by

During the fifties and sixties the increase in highly qualified applicants far outstripped the increase in enrollment, causing headaches, though the pleasurable kind, for the Admissions Office.

growth in the college-age population, increased by 3,500 students to 11,400, with most of the gain in the graduate ranks, and the number of professors from 360 to 935. An important aspect of these unparalleled advances was the increased participation of the Board of Trustees. Their work load became so heavy that, with court approval, they increased their number to 35 from the 15 established by Mrs. Stanford in 1899. In the process the board provided for the direct election of eight members by the alumni and added younger members, members of minorities, and more women.

Sterling moved first to enlarge Stanford's roll of distinguished faculty members. He was determined not to settle for second best, not to rely on California sunshine as a substitute for decent salaries. In the recruitment of faculty he was aided by Frederick E. Terman, appointed vice-president and provost after his success as dean of the School of Engineering. Sterling was sometimes referred to as the architect and Terman the engineer of the growing Stanford. They were sure that an outstanding faculty would attract superior

students and that irresistible pressures for more and better classrooms, laboratories, libraries, and residence halls would inevitably follow—and they were right.

During the Sterling presidency more than 30 major building projects were completed. A new medical center, including a hospital, was built so that the School of Medicine could be transplanted from San Francisco to the campus, and the Graduate School of Business moved from cramped Outer Quad space to its own building. Meyer undergraduate library and the expansion of the Hoover Institution developed to the east of the Quad, and to the west a whole new science area sprang up with facilities for physics, engineering, earth sciences, chemistry, and biology— in the process freeing Quad space for the humanities and social sciences. The Stanford Linear Accelerator Center, with its two-mile-long firing tube, was built in the foothills. Three major dormitories—Florence Moore, Wilbur, and Crothers Memorial—plus Escondido Village for married students and Tresidder Memorial Union strengthened the University's residential character. Bowman

The last of the spindled oak chairs, squeaky and scarred, disappeared from Stanford class-rooms 15 or 20 years ago, replaced by modern armchairs or sleek theater-type seating. With a writing tablet added, the Stanford chair is a first cousin of an ingenious piece of furniture known as the "Douglas Office Chair." Because of its near indestructibility, the Douglas was a favorite all over the pioneer West, as was its cousin with generations of Stanford students.

Alumni House (1952) gave the University's growing body of graduates a home of their own. Faculty, after meeting for years in a little redwood house in the Arboretum followed by several years of no quarters at all, were provided with a handsome clubhouse in 1965. All in all, it was the greatest period of construction since Mrs. Stanford's "stone age" at the turn of the century.

Early in his presidency Sterling turned to development of the Stanford land as an exercise in self-help. It was a move anticipated by the founders. "The endowment of lands," Senator Stanford told the trustees at their first meeting in 1885, "... will insure to the University an income much greater than would be realized were their value to be invested in any reliable, interest-bearing security." The founders had stipulated that the land could not be sold. It could be leased, however, and this was being done for cattle grazing and flower growing when the post-World War II boom in population and the mushrooming electronics industry on the San Francisco Peninsula opened the way for much greater income. The trustees, reserving approximately 5,700 acres for educational purposes—for the most part the central portion running from El Camino Real to the back boundary in the foothills—have allowed development of the outer areas for light industrial, commercial, professional, and residential uses. High standards for architectural control and preservation of open space have been maintained. The leases now yield about $4.6 million a year.

Late in the fifties Sterling organized a group of faculty and staff to lay out the University's academic goals and financial needs for the decade ahead. Because of the Stanford cardinal color of its binding, this study was known

Left: Giant oaks shelter the tarmac in front of Dinkelspiel Auditorium. Below: Bowman Alumni House, made possible through the generosity of Guy C. Bowman, '02, and his wife, is headquarters of the independent, 50,000-member Stanford Alumni Association.

J.E. WALLACE STERLING   Fifth President (1949-1968)

The Sterlings at home.

Wallace Sterling described universities as "engines of change" and it is certainly true that he kept Stanford's motor running. "The very founding of the University expressed a will to venture, to experiment, to innovate," he said. So much happened during the 19 Sterling years that it is sometimes hard to remember that he moved at a deliberate pace, always testing and wrestling with a new idea before accepting it. "Don't be one to have off with the old and on with the new until you have a good look at the new," he cautioned a group of students. In that same talk he told of other simple values he had learned as the son of a clergyman who served in rural Canadian parishes. "It is a story," he said, "of ultimate agreement between father and son about the homely virtues of self-reliance, of hard work as the honest application of talents, whatever they may be, with which each of us is endowed. It is the story of a certain independence of spirit which identifies each of us as an individual, and which makes each of us jealous of the freedom that undergirds our individualism. . . . It is the understanding that Rome was not built in a day, and that, although change is always with us, the great virtues are constant in the midst of change."

as the "Red Book." When Ford Foundation officials came calling in 1959 to talk about a special incentive grant program they had in mind, the Red Book was laid before them and they were impressed. "We had done our homework," Dr. Sterling said.

The Ford Foundation awarded Stanford $25 million on condition that it raise $75 million on its own. This was the root of the PACE campaign which in three years raised $114 million, a new record among private universities. "It was probably this exploit in planning and fund raising that as much as anything else fixed Stanford in the minds of government officials and foundation officers as the most enterprising and innovative university on the West Coast, perhaps in the nation...," it was stated in an essay published by the Carnegie Commission on Higher Education. "By any of the ordinary indices

—growth in facilities or budget, faculty distinction, the test scores of successful applicants, or the American Council on Education ratings of graduate programs—Stanford rose to a place among the best half-dozen American universities and is still, on top of it, a marvelously pleasant place."

The pleasantness was to be temporarily dimmed by the onset of student activism late in the sixties and into the seventies. Dr. Sterling experienced the first wave before becoming chancellor in 1968. He was succeeded in the presidency by Kenneth S. Pitzer, who had been president of Rice University.

Although student militancy captured the headlines and led to the impression that the campus was all but paralyzed, most students continued to attend classes, put on plays, compete in athletics. Professors were teaching, research was progressing. Dr. Pitzer gave

ACADEMICS ABROAD

Wallace Sterling had been immersed in the study of European history and government for some 20 years, first as a Ph.D. student at Stanford and then as a professor at the California Institute of Technology, before he became president of Stanford in 1949. He had also been a news analyst in international affairs for CBS radio for six years and covered the United Nations organizational meetings in San Francisco in 1945.

This experience as scholar-journalist convinced Sterling that America was going to need more young people who were interested in foreign affairs and proficient in foreign languages. So he was in a receptive mood when Friedrich Wilhelm Strothmann, head of the Department of Germanic and Romanic Languages, came to him with his dream of establishing Stanford branch campuses in overseas locations. The dream became reality when the first study center was opened near Stuttgart, Germany, in 1958 with 63 carefully selected students from the home campus in attendance.

Under the direction of Robert A. Walker, professor of political science, the program was soon extended to France, Italy, Austria, and England. Today there are 12 centers with varying programs, located in Berlin, Bonn, Cliveden near London, Florence, Lima, Nairobi, Paris, Rome, Salamanca, Sao Paulo, Tours in France, and Vienna. Mark Mancall, professor of history, succeeded Walker as director in 1973.

The Stanford Overseas Campuses program is designed primarily for undergraduates and over the years some 40 percent of them have taken part, usually for a six-month period. They come from all parts of the University—humanities, social sciences, physical sciences, and engineering. Full academic credit is given for overseas work, tuition is the same as for the home campus, and room and board rates are comparable. Scholarships are continued. Students live either in Stanford facilities, in dormitories of foreign universities, in apartments, or with local families. Teaching is done by Stanford faculty members or scholars from overseas institutions.

"Attending an overseas campus is not a tourist thing," Mancall emphasizes. "Visiting historic sites and museums, going to concerts and plays and pubs, and getting to know local people are all part of the adventure of being in a foreign land, but real engagement with the human, cultural, and physical resources of a foreign society occurs best in the context of academic instruction."

The students seem to agree. One of them, at the conclusion of the first session in Germany in 1958, expressed a sentiment that thousands of students have repeated in their own way since then. "A half year at Stanford-in-Germany is the greatest intellectual stimulation we have ever experienced," she wrote. "We'll all go back to Stanford better students, better Americans, and better human beings."

faculty and students a larger hand in running the University and he strengthened under-graduate education, notably by the addition of the Human Biology Program. Major building projects completed during his term included the Nathan Cummings Art Building, the William F. Durand Building for Space Engineering and Science, the Ruth Wattis Mitchell Earth Sciences Building, and the remodeling of Jordan Hall for the Psychology Department and the west wing of Encina Hall for the Food Research Institute. However, faced with increasing disruption because of the prolonged conflict in Southeast Asia and the resultant difficulty in obtaining "the very broad and active support from all of those groups who together are responsible for the well-being of the University," Dr. Pitzer resigned in 1970.

Richard W. Lyman took office as the University's seventh president in September of 1970. Having served as vice-president and provost for three years, he was steeled to coping with campus activism and during the next two years he presided over not the elimination of protest but its rechanneling into nondestructive forms. "A comfortable university is virtually a contradiction in terms," he reminded those who longed for something more like total victory. "We exist to disturb and activate the minds of men and women."

Dr. Lyman decided against a formal presidential inauguration. A natural communicator, he elected instead to take his message personally to students, faculty, alumni, and the public in a rapid-fire series of talks and question-and-answer sessions. His message: "We certainly have our shortcomings, and it is healthy for us to recognize that fact. But Stanford *is* a great university." And he emphasized that there is nothing wrong with the

KENNETH SANBORN PITZER
Sixth President (1968-1970)

Kenneth Sanborn Pitzer didn't shrink from expressing to people what he thought was right, even if it was something they didn't want to hear. He did so, during the days of campus activism, with students, faculty, trustees, and alumni. But, as it turned out, some of the things he said to his fellow scientists were of more lasting importance. A distinguished chemist at UC-Berkeley before serving as president of Rice University and then coming to Stanford, Pitzer was awarded the prestigious Priestley Medal by the American Chemical Society in 1969. "Ever since the time of Francis Bacon we have held a sort of laissez-faire theory that scientific knowledge would automatically yield economic and social progress," he said in his acceptance speech. This was wrong, he said. As soon as an application of basic research can be visualized, "one should ask not only 'Is it possible?' but also 'Is it desirable?' And the desirability should be judged from a humanistic as well as an economic basis."

kind of elitism that goes with excellence: "There is a world of difference between unfair and entrenched privilege on the one hand and earned quality on the other."

Beginning in 1969 and continuing through the turbulent times, planning had been quietly going forward on a new capital fund drive. Inflation and a declining securities market had created serious financial problems. Rigorous cost control came first; in a series of planned moves several millions of dollars were stripped from the budget base. Then, with economic conditions improving and campus radicalism cooling, a five-year drive was kicked off in April of 1972. It was called "The Campaign for Stanford"—a refreshing disregard for euphemism. University officers had recommended a goal of $260 million. The trustees, taking a hard look at projected needs, decided to go for $300 million, the most ambitious goal ever set by a university. At the end of the allotted five years, thanks to 5,000 volunteers and 54,000 donors, the goal was topped at $304 million.

The largest share—$132 million—was raised for the University's permanent endowment fund, the reliable base for a private institution's financing. More than $57 million was obtained for filling the building gaps that remained after the "second stone age" of the fifties and sixties. The campaign contributed in some measure toward many projects. Major examples are the de Guerre Pools and Courts, the Seeley G. Mudd Chemistry Building, the Frederick E. Terman Engineering Center, the Herbert Hoover Memorial Building, Crown Quadrangle (the Law School complex), the Cecil H. Green Library, three Row houses (two of them named for their donor, Robert S. Moore) for student living, the reconstruction of Outer Quad buildings,

and, at the Medical Center, the Sherman Fairchild Science Building and Auditorium, the Louis B. Mayer Cancer Research Laboratory, and a major addition to the hospital.

Campaign benefits were felt in all parts of the campus. There were 49 endowed professorships when the drive started, 125 when it was completed. Gifts of scholarships, fellowships, and student loan funds topped $35 million and the level of term support for instruction, research, and other uses was raised from $15 million to $20 million annually.

When he took the job of president, Lyman pointed out that universities change only gradually. Some things did happen more rapidly than he expected—the stronger position of ethnic minorities and women as faculty and students, albeit a problem far from solved, is one example; the increase in bureaucracy

Since the University's earliest days, Stanford students have expressed their feelings, sometimes peaceably, sometimes not, about a wide variety of issues, from a 1908 order forbidding students "to visit saloons" (which led to a small rebellion and the suspension of 132 men) to a proposed reinstitution of the military draft in 1979.

Dick and Jing Lyman at Rose Bowl festivities.

RICHARD W. LYMAN, Seventh President (1970-1980)

The economics of running a university were shifting rapidly when Richard Lyman took office in 1970. Inflation was closing out an era in which new money was readily available to undertake new programs. Since then, if something new was to be added, something old had to be trimmed or cut. "That's the challenge we now face," Lyman told an interviewer, "to go on being creative, have a place that's vividly alive, without being able to grow to any considerable degree." At budget time administrators had to

defend their requests for pieces of the finite pie, and they found Lyman a hard sell. A colleague said, "Dick Lyman expects argument, welcomes argument, enjoys it, fights to win, doesn't mind losing a good

fight." His articulate, "think-on-my-feet" style was often brought into play at question-and-answer sessions with students and alumni, and they liked it, even when they disagreed with him.

to deal with government regulation is another.

"But in basic essentials," he told an alumni audience in 1979, "Stanford has evolved slowly, and on a more or less predictable, steady course.

"We remain very selective in both what we undertake to do and whom we ask to do it, whether faculty or students or staff.

"We remain medium sized; total enrollments have not changed significantly for more than a decade, though there have been some shifts in the composition of the student body.

"We remain better off financially than many institutions yet not well enough off to enable responsible administrators to sleep very soundly when they've spent the day looking at financial projections in an inflationary era.

"We remain concerned to sustain a powerful alternative to California's excellent system of state-supported higher education.

"And we proceed into the 1980s knowing that we don't always attain excellence, but that we'll be doomed the day we stop aspiring to it."

During the summer of 1980 Lyman left Stanford to become president of the Rockefeller Foundation, the fourth largest philanthropic organization in the nation. He had been a member of the foundation's board since 1976 and served as chairman of its Commission on the Humanities. He was also chairman of the executive committee of the American Association of Universities.

Donald Kennedy was named Stanford's eighth president on the eve of the 1980 commencement weekend. Holder of three degrees from Harvard, Kennedy joined the Stanford faculty in biology in 1960. His research in the small networks of nerve cells earned him membership in the National Academy of Sciences. For his superb teaching, graduating seniors asked him to speak at Class Day a record three times. At the 1976 commencement he received the Lloyd W. Dinkelspiel Award for his teaching and research and for developing the pathbreaking interdisciplinary Human Biology Program. On leave in 1977-79, he served as commissioner of the Food and Drug Administration in Washington, returning to Stanford as vice-president and provost.

Kennedy, born in 1931, is a lean six-footer, a fly fisherman and skier who, like his predecessor, bicycles to the office. He can be blunt when the occasion demands but is a friendly, accessible administrator who brings out the best in other people. He is, said retiring President Lyman at commencement, "someone with truly formidable talent, energy, and devotion to this institution."

DONALD KENNEDY, Eighth President (1980-)

Map Key

(Uses listed are current uses. For former uses and other information, see Building Inventory, page 223. For map of Inner and Outer Quads, see page 44.)

1. **Cowell Student Health Center.**
2. **Wilbur Hall.** Student residence.
3. **Escondido Village.** Student residences.
4. **Bing Nursery School.**
5. **Branner Hall.** Student residence.
6. **Toyon Hall.** Student residence.
7. **Eating Club Building.**
8. **Fire and Police Station.**
9. **Roscoe Maples Pavilion.** Basketball and other athletics.
10. **Dorothy and Sidney de Guerre Pools and Courts.**
11. **Stanford Stadium.**
12. **Encina Gymnasium.**
13. **Athletics, Physical Education and Recreation Building.**
14. **Old Pavilion** (formerly Encina Pavilion). Facilities Office; Planning; Facilities Engineering; Personnel.
15. **Encina Hall.** Vice-President for Business and Finance; Vice-President for Development; Economics; Food Research Institute.
16. **Encina Commons.** Business and Finance; The Station (restaurant); Economics.
17. **Crothers Hall.** Primarily law students' residence.
18. **Crothers Memorial Hall.** Primarily engineering students' residence.
19. **Stern Hall.** Student residence.
20. **Crown Quadrangle (Law School)**
    a. Robert Crown Library.
    b. F.I.R. Hall.
    c. James Irvine Gallery.
    d. Kresge Auditorium.
21. **Post Office.**
22. **Stanford Bookstore.**
23. **Center for Educational Research at Stanford (CERAS).**
24. **Career Planning and Placement Center.**
25. **J. Henry Meyer Memorial Library.** Undergraduate library.
26. **School of Education** (includes Cubberley Auditorium).

27. **Cecil H. Green Library** (formerly Main Library). Library administration; humanities and social sciences collections; general reference; Special Collections; University Archives; Government Documents; Technical Services.
28. **Nathan Cummings Art Building** (includes Annenberg Auditorium).
29. **Thomas Welton Stanford Art Gallery.**
30. **Hoover Institution on War, Revolution and Peace.**
    a. Hoover Tower.
    b. Lou Henry Hoover Building.
    c. Herbert Hoover Memorial Building.
31. **Memorial Hall** (includes Memorial Auditorium and Little Theater). Drama; KZSU radio station.
32. **Graduate School of Business** (includes Bishop Auditorium).
33. **Old Steam Plant.** Stanford Band; storage.
34. **Galvez House.** Sponsored Projects.
35. **Terman Engineering Laboratory.** Mechanical Engineering.
36. **Havas Engineering Building.** Applied Mechanics.
37. **Civil Engineering** (formerly Durand Laboratory). Civil Engineering; Research Coordination (engineering).
38. **John Blume Earthquake Center.**
39. **Peterson Laboratory.** Materials Science and Engineering; Applied Earth Sciences.
40. **Stanford University Press.**
41. **Storke Student Publications Building.**
42. **News and Publications Service; Public Events.**
43. **Word Graphics.**
44. **High Temperature Gasdynamics Laboratory.**
45. **Building 610.** Engineering student shops.

46. **Old Firehouse.** Student organizations.
47. **Old Union.** Registrar; Counseling and Testing Center; Admissions; Graduate Studies; Student Affairs; Undergraduate Studies; Undergraduate Financial Aid; Overseas Studies.
48. **Building 590.** The Nitery; Stanford Center for Innovation in Research and Education (SCIRE); Stanford Workshops on Political and Social Issues (SWOPSI); Undergraduate Special Courses; Graduate Studies; Chicano Fellows.
49. **The Clubhouse.** Student organizations; Volunteers in Asia; United Campus Ministries.
50. **Music Building** (includes Dinkelspiel Auditorium).
51. **Tresidder Memorial Union.** Associated Students of Stanford University (ASSU); recreation, conference, and commercial services.
52. **Bowman Alumni House.** Stanford Alumni Association.
53. **Stanford Faculty Club.**
54. **Bechtel International Center.** Services for foreign students and faculty.
55. **Florence Moore Hall.** Student residence.
56. **The Knoll.** Music.
57. **Lou Henry Hoover House.** The University president's house.
58. **Boathouse.**
59. **Roble Hall.** Student residence.
60. **Lagunita Court.** Student residence.
61. **Frederick E. Terman Engineering Center.** Dean of Engineering; Civil Engineering; Industrial Engineering and Engineering Management; Design

Division of Mechanical Engineering; Operations Research; Engineering-Economics Systems.
62. **Roble Gymnasium** (formerly Women's Gymnasium).
63. **Ruth Wattis Mitchell Earth Sciences Building.** Dean of Earth Sciences; Applied Earth Sciences; Petroleum Engineering; Geophysics.
64. **William F. Durand Building for Space Engineering and Science.** Aeronautics and Astronautics; Applied Mechanics.
65. **Hugh H. Skilling Building.** Engineering.
66. **Lloyd Noble Petroleum Engineering Building.**
67. **Henry Salvatori Laboratory of Geophysics.**
68. **Applied Electronics Laboratory (AEL).**
69. **Electronics Research Laboratory (ERL).**
70. **Jack A. McCullough Building.** Electrical Engineering; Center for Materials Research.
71. **Physics Lecture Hall.**
72. **Russell H. Varian Laboratory of Physics.**
73. **High Energy Physics Laboratory.**
74. **Sequoia Hall** (formerly Roble Hall). Statistics.
75. **William F. Herrin Hall.** Biological Sciences.
76. **William F. Herrin Laboratories.** Biological Sciences.
77. **Old Chemistry Building.**
78. **Stauffer Chemical Engineering Building.**
79. **Stauffer Physical Chemistry Building.**
80. **Stauffer Organic Chemistry Building.**
81. **Organic Chemistry Laboratory.**

82. **Seeley G. Mudd Chemistry Building.**
83. **Stanford Museum of Art** (formerly Leland Stanford Junior Museum).
84. **Stanford Family Mausoleum.**
85. **Stanford Barn.** Commercial shops.
86. **Stanford Medical Center.**
    a. Stanford University Hospital.
    b. Hoover Pavilion (formerly Palo Alto Hospital).
    c. School of Medicine; Stanford University Clinics.
    d. Anatomy/Medical Microbiology Building.
    e. Sherman Fairchild Science Building (includes Sherman Fairchild Auditorium).
    f. Louis B. Mayer Cancer Biology Research Laboratory.
87. **Ventura Hall** (formerly Casa Ventura). Institute for Mathematical Studies in the Social Sciences (IMSSS).
88. **Serra House.** Center for Research on Women (CROW).
89. **Applied Physics Building.**
90. **Edward L. Ginzton Laboratory** (formerly Microwave Laboratory). Microwave research.
91. **Jordan Quad.** Communication (until 1982); Stanford Center for Information Processing (SCIP); Institute for Mathematical Studies in the Social Sciences (IMSSS); Research Libraries Group-Research Libraries Information Network (RLG-RLIN).
92. **George Forsythe Hall.** Stanford Center for Information Processing (SCIP).
93. **Red Barn.** Stanford Riding School.
94. **Stanford Golf Course.**
95. **Stanford Linear Accelerator Center.**

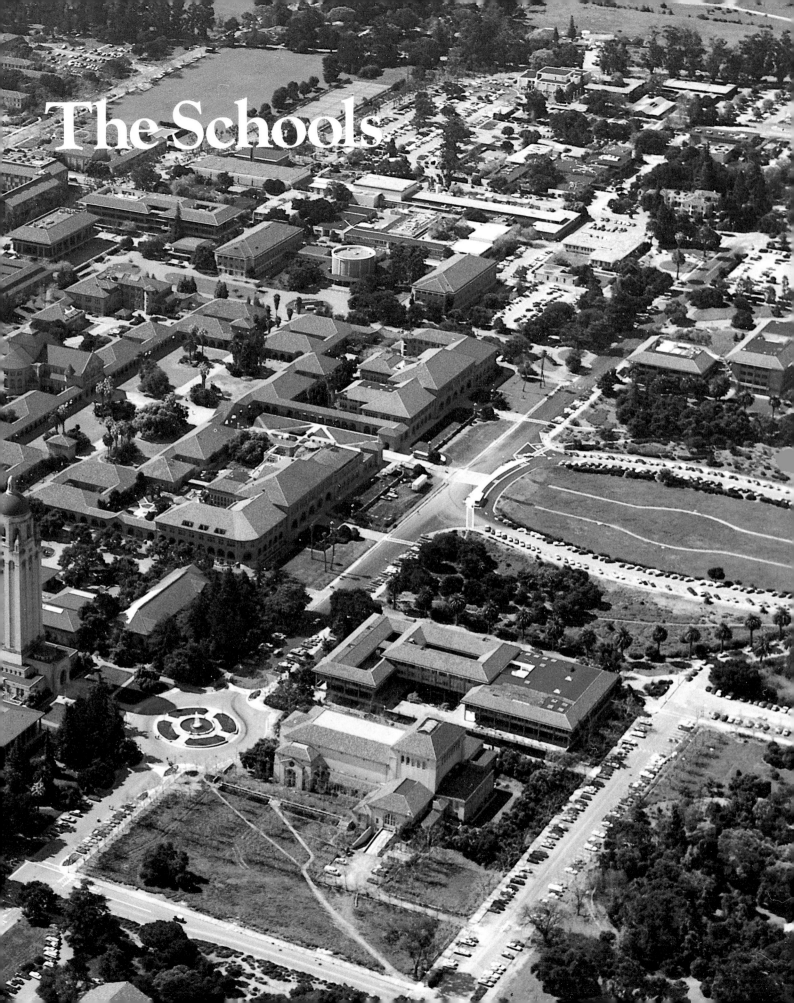

The Schools

Humanities and Sciences

At the time of Stanford's founding, American higher education was gradually breaking away from the rigid curriculum of classical studies, without electives, that every student was obliged to follow. President Jordan, never given to pedagogical caution, decided to jump the traces entirely. He opened Stanford's doors with a freewheeling major-subject system. The University was not organized in schools, only departments—21 of them in the principal areas of humanities, social studies, science, and technology. Each entering freshman selected one department as his field of specialization. English I (Art of Writing) was the only course required of all students and major-subject requirements were not to take more than one-third of the student's program; the rest was to be filled by electives.

The Stanford system emphasized the independence, initiative, and responsibility of the student. "It attracted to Stanford University more than a normal proportion of free spirits," noted Registrar Elliott.

When Ray Lyman Wilbur became president in 1916, he recognized that the system needed some tuning up. He wrote in his memoirs: "The old departmental system had begun crystallizing into airtight compartments, so that we had to break down some of the barriers to get a freer circulation of air, a wider view, and more opportunities for interchange of ideas and information."

The key to breaking down the barriers lay in grouping the departments with related interests into schools, but change of this magnitude does not happen quickly in a university setting. "There is always quite a herd of sacred cows browsing about in the academic field," Wilbur observed. Delay was also caused by World War I, so that it was not until 1922

that the School of Biological Sciences, the first of the nonprofessional schools, was formed. During the next three years existing departments were shaped into the Schools of Social Sciences, Physical Sciences, and Letters (the latter was broadened in 1942 to the School of Humanities).

This pattern prevailed until after World War II when it was decided that the narrowness which once afflicted the departments had overtaken the schools. Knowledge had become even more interdependent, demanding a broader approach for the undergraduate, to be followed by specialization at the graduate level. Accordingly, in 1948 the Schools of Humanities, Biological Sciences, Social Sciences, and Physical Sciences were joined in the School of Humanities and Sciences.

While retaining the functions of research and advanced instruction, the new school set

Professor J. Dirk Walecka, chairman of the Physics Department, has championed the importance of teaching ability in the selection and promotion of faculty members.

Right: The John Stauffer Laboratory for Physical Chemistry. Below: A laboratory in the old Chemistry Building after a 1960s refurbishing.

Free form has changed art—and art classes. Above: In this 1895 class, one student wears her mortarboard. Right: Professor Keith Boyle teaches a class in a Cummings Art Building studio.

The Physics Lecture Hall is known to the students as the "Physics Tank."

about to give the undergraduate a stronger dose of liberal or general education. "Students ought [to acquire], we believe," said Clarence H. Faust, the first dean of humanities and sciences, ". . . a sufficient grasp of social, economic, and political problems to exercise intelligent judgment as responsible citizens; sufficient understanding of the modes of operation of the scientist to live intelligently in a scientific age; and a sufficient competence in understanding and appreciating literature and the arts not to be reduced to the comic book and the soap opera for enjoyment."

Today the School of Humanities and Sciences offers more than three-fourths of the units taken by Stanford undergraduates and one-third of those taken by graduates. It includes 34 departments and programs:

African and Afro-American Studies
Anthropology
Applied Physics
Art
Asian Languages
Biological Sciences
Chemistry
Classics
Communication
Comparative Literature
Computer Science
Drama
Economics
English
Food Research Institute
French and Italian
German Studies
History
Human Biology
Humanities Special Programs
Latin American Studies
Linguistics
Mathematics
Modern Thought and Literature
Music
Philosophy
Physics
Political Science
Psychology
Religious Studies
Slavic Languages and Literature
Sociology
Spanish and Portuguese
Statistics

Russell Varian (left) and Sigurd Varian with big and little versions of klystron tubes.

THE KLYSTRON CONNECTION

Russell and Sigurd Varian came to Stanford University in 1937 with an idea and a creative urge. The University, financially strapped by the Depression, appointed them research associates without salary in the Department of Physics, set them up with basement laboratory space, and gave them $100 a year for materials and supplies.

Within seven months the Varians had conceived and built a device that was to make airborne radar feasible, thus helping to crush Hitler's Luftwaffe and destroy the German submarine fleet in World War II. In the postwar period their invention, the klystron tube, became a cornerstone for microwave research and development throughout the world.

Russell, who had earned two degrees in physics at Stanford in the mid-twenties, was

the theorist. Incorporating a cavity resonator newly invented by William W. Hansen, a brilliant young faculty member, Russell worked out the tube's design on paper. Sigurd, a skilled mechanic and former Pan American Airways pilot, built the prototype tube, Model A. (The improved Model B is now in the Smithsonian Institution.) The brothers named their creation klystron, from the Greek verb 'klyzo,' expressing the breaking of waves on the beach, a metaphorical reference to the critical bunching of electrons in the tube.

The klystron turned out to be more than an important wartime development. Edward L. Ginzton, who worked with the Varians as a graduate student assistant, has written: "It helped make commercial air navigation safe, it opened the possibility of worldwide communications by satellites, and it led to a variety of high-energy particle accelerators useful in medicine and in nuclear physics." The brothers established Varian Associates in 1948, and the firm soon became the first to build in the Stanford Industrial Park. Ginzton was appointed a professor at Stanford in 1946 but left in 1959 to become chairman of the board of Varian Associates.

When the Varians began their experiments on the campus, they agreed to share financial returns with the University. Stanford has received more than $2.5 million in klystron royalties, a large part of which was used in the construction of the Russell H. Varian Laboratory of Physics, dedicated in 1962. Russell died of a heart attack in 1959 while on an Alaskan cruise, and Sigurd perished in a private plane crash off the coast of Mexico in 1961.

"The school is what a university is all about, only more so; it is the part of Stanford most involved in the creation and preservation of knowledge," believes Halsey L. Royden, who was appointed dean in 1973. (Royden is a mathematician whose research interest is the function of complex variables—appropriate training for overseeing such a complicated organization as H&S, as it is commonly known.) Because H&S offers both undergraduate and graduate work, with many classes overlapping the two, undergraduates can go as far as they want or are able, and senior faculty teach beginning as well as advanced courses.

Departments of the school fare well in national ratings. "Several are considered to be the best of their kind," Dean Royden comments, "and most are in the top half dozen. There is open water between our Psychology and Computer Science Departments and their nearest competitors." But he adds that

Margery Bailey, an actress as well as a professor, made Dickens and Shakespeare pulse with life for her English classes. She died in 1963 after 50 years as a Stanford student and teacher.

A consummate teacher of short story writing, Edith Mirrielees tempered criticism with gentleness. She was an active faculty member from 1910 to 1944 and an editor until her death in 1962.

Harold C. Schmidt, professor of music, emeritus, directed the Memorial Church choir for 28 years and is much acclaimed for his dramatic leading of the Stanford Hymn at Commencement. His gifted direction and knowledge of classical scores raised the Stanford chorus to a professional level.

A familiar figure in History Corner for more than 40 years, Thomas A. Bailey was head of the History Department from 1952 to 1955 and held the Margaret Byrne Professorship in American History from 1952 until his retirement in 1968. Among his 15 books, Diplomatic History of the American People had been published in nine editions.

he is inclined to take these rankings with "a small pinch of salt" because of the difficulty of putting a quantitative measure on what are essentially qualitative endeavors.

If the School of Humanities and Sciences is the core of the University academically, it is also at the center architecturally. Except for Geology Corner and offices of the president and the provost, the entire Inner and Outer Quads are occupied by the school. "As other schools moved to their own new buildings off the Quad, we got the hand-me-downs," the dean says. "But they're such gorgeous hand-me-downs that we're not complaining." Several H&S departments, notably those requiring large laboratory or studio space, are located outside the Quad.

The great breadth of the school's curriculum paves the way for the interdisciplinary approach demanded by the state of civilization.

"It is pointless," President Lyman once declared, "to imagine that problems as complex and full of intricate relationships as, say, the problem of the ghetto are going to yield to uncoordinated assaults by traditional academic specialties." Universities, he said, must offer "ways of bringing many scholarly disciplines to bear on such issues."

One such program of Humanities and Sciences, the Human Biology Program, has become one of the University's most popular

Eleanor E. Maccoby, Barbara Kimball Browning Professor of Humanities and Sciences, is the second woman to be appointed to an endowed chair at Stanford. Professor of psychology and head of the department from 1973 to 1976, Maccoby is renowned both for her research on the social and intellectual development of children and for her teaching excellence.

The Knoll, built in 1918 on rising ground near Lake Lagunita as the residence of the University president, has been occupied for many years by the Music Department.

Left: The chemistry building Mrs. Stanford erected on the Oval. Below: Memorial Hall seat of the Drama Department. The hall honors the memory of Stanford students, faculty, and alumni who lost their lives in the two world wars.

John McCarthy, professor of computer science and director of the Stanford Artificial Intelligence Laboratory, is a pioneer in research dealing with artificial intelligence and is responsible for the LISP language used in that field.

James Lowell Gibbs Jr., well known to students for his quick wit, is professor of anthropology and is actively involved in the African and Afro-American Studies Programs. He was dean of undergraduate studies from 1971 to 1976.

Approximately 125 musical performances are held in Dinkelspiel Auditorium each year. Right: Biology students explore along the bank of Lake Lagunita.

majors. It responds to the need for knowledge of the complex relationship of man with nature, exemplified by the dilemmas of social policy in health and education, population problems, pollution of the environment, and conservation and development of natural resources. Professors from nine H&S departments, joined by others from the faculties of Law, Business, Engineering, and Medicine, teach in the program. Other examples of this crossing of lines are found in the programs in African and Afro-American studies, American studies, medieval studies, and international relations.

Early in 1980 the Senate of the Academic Council adopted a new Western culture requirement for freshmen, the greatest change in Stanford's undergraduate curriculum in a decade. Entering students will be able to choose from four or more separate, year-long course sequences, sharing a core group of great works from such sources as Plato, Homer, Dante, Galileo, Voltaire, Marx, Freud, Darwin, and the Bible (which has a familiar ring to those who remember the Western Civilization course which all freshmen took for many years until it was a victim in the late sixties of the fashion to drop course requirements).

Said history professor Lewis W. Spitz during consideration of the new requirement: "I admire science and engineering, but they should not exclude everything else from a young person's mind. What a terrible world it would be if those who command the heights of technocracy—who are capable of blowing us all to bits, or polluting our globe, or splicing genes to make new forms of life—know only exponential curves and printouts and test tubes. All we ask is that they leave a window open to the wider world of humanity."

Chilton R. "Chick" Bush, head of the Journalism Department for 27 years, was a pioneer in communications research and opinion polling. He arranged one of the nation's first on-the-job training programs for budding journalists and his book, Newspaper Reporting of Public Affairs, *is the standard in its field. Bush died in 1972.*

N. Scott Momaday, professor of English, received the Pulitzer Prize for his first novel, House Made of Dawn, *in 1969, the first American Indian to receive this honor. Momaday received his master's and Ph.D. degrees from Stanford and joined the faculty in 1972. He has narrated several films about American Indian heritage, including the 1978 award-winning documentary* More Than Bows and Arrows.

The Stanford Solar Observatory, in a sheltered foothill spot, continuously observes the sun's magnetic field.

A WILDERNESS JEWEL

The Jasper Ridge Biological Preserve is a jewel beyond price. Its 1,300 acres, which anchor the western extreme of the University's landholdings, form a richly variegated wilderness enclave that is within easy daily reach of Stanford students and researchers.

Faculty members in the natural sciences who came West in 1891 to help found the University soon discovered that Jasper Ridge, which takes its name from the reddish rock that underlies much of its area, is a superb resource. It en-, compasses nine distinct biological environments —grassland, chaparral, open oak woodland, broadleafed forest, redwood forest, stream bank (along San Francisquito Creek), freshwater swamp, marsh, and lake (Searsville). A class can pass through all nine in a single afternoon. In addition, a long blade of serpentine outcrop at the height of the ridge supports only severely adapted plants, untouched by importations, in its calcium-deficient soil.

Because of its unusual bunching of plant communities, the ridge contains 84 of the 162 vascular plant families that grow in California, and, of the plant communities that exist in the Coast Range of Central California, only the three oceanfront communities are missing.

The preserve gives refuge to a large and varied animal population, including coyotes, bobcats, deer, rodents, reptiles, butterflies, and birds. A rare horned toad exists there and several birds that seldom breed in this part of the state are numerous within the protective tangles of the chaparral.

Since the mid-sixties there has been a surge in the use of Jasper Ridge for teaching and research. This is due in part to the general awakening to critical environmental problems and to the development in the Department of Biological Sciences, which administers the preserve, of a strong program in population biology.

Approximately 200 students a year are enrolled in 19 graduate and undergraduate courses that use Jasper Ridge for field work. Graduate students also conduct research there; the first Ph.D. based on Jasper research was awarded in 1897.

Paul Ehrlich, noted Stanford population biologist, and his associates have for 20 years used a colony of checkerspot butterflies in studies of population dynamics. Professors Harold A. Mooney and Jonathan Roughgarden, who have also based research on the ridge, have joined with Ehrlich in developing a computer model that will predict the effectiveness of the strategies that plants of the preserve use in capturing the energies available to them. The natural way plants have of warding off insect predators is one aspect of the study.

Because of the growth of population on the San Francisco Peninsula and the need to protect scientific instruments, screens, markers, etc., installed on the site, the University has found it necessary to secure Jasper Ridge from public access. Recreational use of Searsville Lake, begun in 1922 by Ernie Brandsten, Stanford swimming coach, was terminated in 1976. But a very vigorous docent program, staffed by Stanford students and residents of surrounding communities, guides about 2,500 persons a year through the preserve. Jasper Ridge is also used by students from most Bay Area colleges and universities and by groups of school children.

Earth Sciences

Geologist Irwin Remson—powerfully built, still trim in his mid-fifties—leaned back in his office chair. Behind him, through the huge corner windows of his third-floor room in the Mitchell Earth Sciences Building, stretched a dazzling panorama of red-tiled roofs.

"When I got concerned enough about the degradation of our environment to want to do something about it," he said, "I decided that as a scientist and teacher I could have the most impact by training the people who might affect the environment as planners and decision makers. I wanted to get scientists and engineers to go into the environmental field as a specialty, and I wanted to get some science and engineering into the people who were going into management."

The result is the very successful undergraduate Environmental Earth Sciences Program taught by Remson and George Mader, a practicing city and regional planner. The program is built around a year-long course during which students prepare a comprehensive land-use plan for a Bay Area community. They must finally present the plan and defend it at a meeting of that city's officials.

Environmental majors take other earth sciences courses and a wide selection of classes in such related fields as engineering, biology, chemistry, and computer science. They also study the social sciences, humanities, and fine arts. "An environmentalist cannot function without a civic conscience and a sense of beauty," Remson believes. Graduates of the program go on to advanced degrees in geology and other sciences, engineering, urban planning, landscape architecture, law, business, and even medicine. This is the diffusion of influence that Remson had in mind from the beginning.

Man's influence on the physical environment—and the need to understand the many chain reactions that are being set in motion—is cited by Richard Jahns, who served as dean of the school from 1965 until his return in 1979 to teaching and research, as one of the three areas of change that have revolutionized the earth sciences. Another is the concept of plate tectonics, which Jahns calls the most important development in earth sciences in the past 100 years. It asserts that the entire surface of the earth is composed of 16 or so slowly shifting coastal plates that ride on the hotter and less rigid material lying beneath them. Volcanic "rims of fire," mid-ocean rifts, continental borders, earthquake fault lines, and mountain ranges mark the edges of the plates.

"Plate tectonics," Jahns observes, "for the first time gives us an integrated view of what's been happening to the outer shell of the earth during past geologic time, especially in the

A dazzling collection of over 200 mineral specimens, made possible by Edward Swoboda of Southern California, is on display in the Ruth Wattis Mitchell Earth Sciences Building. It is one of the finest university mineral collections in the world.

Professor Konrad Krauskopf (white hair), chairman of the Geology Department before retiring in 1976, conducted many classes on the Jasper Ridge Biological Preserve. Opposite: The Ruth Wattis Mitchell Earth Sciences Building. Below: A summer field trip to the Klamath in 1895. Pat Silverthorn, on the right, was the Indian guide.

A. Myra Keen, professor of paleontology and malacology, emeritus, was the first woman to receive the prestigious Fellows Medal of the California Academy of Sciences. She was the curator of Stanford's massive shell collection for over 30 years and her book, Sea Shells of Tropical Western America, is a classic.

last 200 million years. Clearly, the earth is a lively planet."

The paleomagnetic research of Allan V. Cox, who succeeded Jahns as dean in 1979, has been fundamental in the development of the plate tectonics concept. Cox, holder of the Cecil H. and Ida M. Green endowed professorship in geophysics, received the Vetlesen Prize, considered the Nobel of earth sciences, in 1971.

The third area of action for the earth sciences cited by Jahns is the endless search for materials and for energy sources, with the one goading the other. "It takes energy to discover and extract materials; it takes materials to produce usable energy," he points out. "And to add to the problem, most of the world's mineral deposits that are readily accessible have been discovered. We have to go deeper, in more exotic places, and learn to deal with lower-grade sources."

Not by accident, the School of Earth Sciences is abreast of all three of these major developments, a fact reflected in the growth of enrollment during Jahns's tenure to about 400 students from a third of that number. During the same period Stanford has been number one or tied for number two among universities chosen by National Science Foundation predoctoral fellows in earth sciences.

"One thing we have insisted on, along with work on the existing frontiers, is sound coverage of the basics," Jahns comments. "You can't get by without them. That's why our program has always been solidly field oriented."

The 180 or so courses now offered in earth sciences are quite a contrast to the seven announced for the Geology Department in the first Stanford catalog, issued for 1891-92. Four of these were taught by John Casper Branner, the first man to be offered a Stanford professorship by David Starr Jordan, his old Cornell classmate. "I would rather work under you as President than any other man alive," Dr. Branner replied. But, having been recently appointed head of the Geological Survey of Arkansas, he demurred at the $4,000 annual salary offered. Jordan promptly raised it to $5,000 and Branner arranged to come early in 1892. Branner became one of the nation's most distinguished geologists, and he succeeded Jordan as president of the University in 1913.

"Upon Dr. Branner's arrival I came under the spell of a great scientist and a great teacher," wrote Herbert Hoover, a somewhat chubby freshman in that first year of Stanford's existence. Hoover was his mentor's office assistant as well as student, and he met his future wife, Lou Henry, in a geology lab.

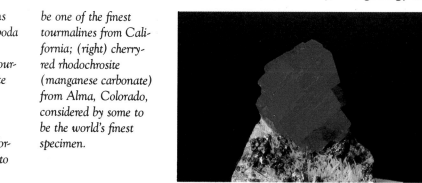

Two of the specimens in the Edward Swoboda Mineral Collection: (left) multicolored tourmaline (a borosilicate mineral), mined by Swoboda out of his Tourmaline Queen Mine in Pala, California, and considered to be one of the finest tourmalines from California; (right) cherry-red rhodochrosite (manganese carbonate) from Alma, Colorado, considered by some to be the world's finest specimen.

Hoover and others who were with or followed him during Stanford's earlier years pioneered in the large-scale development of the natural resources of the world. They set the school's tradition for a close-knit and loyal alumni body.

When Branner came to Stanford in 1892 his professional library was so big he had to bring it in a freight car. He installed it in the geology building on the Inner Quad and made it freely available to his students. He continued to buy books at his own expense and when, at his retirement in 1915, he sold the library to the University it contained 10,000 volumes, an equal number of pamphlets, and many maps. It is the nucleus of today's Branner Earth Sciences Library, one of the finest in the world.

The Department of Mining was added in the University's second year and was joined with the Department of Geology to form the School of Mineral Sciences (later changed to Earth Sciences) in 1947. Eliot Blackwelder, an eminent geologist and National Academy of Sciences member, had headed the Geology Department for 22 years before his retirement in 1945.

The Ruth Wattis Mitchell Earth Sciences Building near Geology Corner on the Outer Quad was erected in 1970. Its 63,000 square feet include classrooms, offices, the Branner library, and—in basement and subbasement levels—a series of laboratories. Mrs. Mitchell, the principal donor, said at the time her gift was announced, "Life has been good to me, and Stanford has been good to my family. Being able to offer something in return is a personal privilege. This building and its facilities will enable Stanford to remain in the vanguard in the education of young men and women who will be tomorrow's leaders."

DANDELIONS UNDER THE SEA

On a deep-sea expedition along the Galapagos Rift in 1977, geology professor Tjeerd van Andel and two companions were the first to locate shimmering underwater hot springs that support a profusion of life on the otherwise barren ocean floor, 10,000 feet down. Clustering around the plumes of warm water were forests of blood-red tube worms—some 12 feet long—unknown organisms in the shape of yellow puff balls that the scientists called "dandelions," and other exotic life forms.

But van Andel and his coworkers were more concerned with the geological story that the warm springs could tell. They are formed when seawater penetrates fissures along the Galapagos Rift at the boundary of two of the massive, slowly shifting plates that are believed to make up all of the earth's crust. Heated in a basaltic layer to about 300°C, the water is forced up through vents, gradually cooling and bringing with it a bacteria-based food supply. The geologists were also intrigued by lava that had hardened over large areas into ruffled sheets, rather than into the piles of pillow-like rock that usually result from volcanic action on the ocean bottom.

Van Andel, a native of the Netherlands and formerly on the staff of the Scripps Institution of Oceanography, joined the Stanford faculty in 1976, the year before the first Galapagos Rift expedition. A second expedition took place early in 1979 and the Stanford oceanographer and his colleagues came back awash in data that promise, on analysis, to add much to their understanding of the earth's processes.

Education

At one end of the long reading room of the Cubberley Library in the School of Education Building, a custom-made glass-enclosed bookcase contains neat rows of textbooks of uniform size and binding. Their bookplates read: "Riverside Textbooks in Education. Foundation Stones of the School of Education Building and the Cubberley Library." Behind this curious inscription lies an unusual story of educational philanthropy.

It is the story of a talented but unassuming dean of education whose Stanford salary peaked at $8,000 in 1933, the year he retired. Unbeknownst to his colleagues, Ellwood Patterson Cubberley had parlayed his earnings from writing and editing into a sizable fortune, and one month after he retired he and his wife turned over to a surprised University stocks and bonds valued at $367,000. Subsequent gifts more than doubled this amount. Thus did books become the "foundation stones" for the Stanford education building and library.

Cubberley came to Stanford as an assistant professor of education in the summer of 1898. The department had been established in 1891 as one of the University's original 21 departments, but the work had languished. Two months after his arrival, when it became certain that one of the three faculty members would not return in the fall, the youthful Cubberley was appointed head of the department. President Jordan called him in and told him that the program was in disrepute and that a majority of the Stanford faculty thought it should be discontinued. He gave Cubberley three years to make it respectable.

"That was a challenge that called up all the fighting blood in me," Cubberley recalled later. He and the other remaining professor quickly turned the department around. The

Above: The Center for Educational Research at Stanford (CERAS) houses most of the School of Education's research activities. It is also the home of the Low Overhead Time-sharing System, which provides interactive computer service to 3,000 undergraduates. Opposite: Cubberley Library.

quality of teaching improved, the number of majors jumped from 43 to 60, and in 1901, the deadline year, a third professor was authorized to share the load.

Since 1891 the department had operated in one small room on the Inner Quad. Into its 23-by-26-foot space were crammed the desks and chairs of the three professors, the "library" of 600 books, and a small table for seminars. The department moved to larger Inner Quad quarters in 1903, with separate offices for each professor, and in 1912 it expanded into adjoining space, providing for more staff and a library of 20,000 volumes.

By the mid-1930s there was again a desperate need for space. The Cubberleys directed that the largest part of their gift was to be used to erect the School of Education Building and to buy books for the large new library on the second floor. With his usual meticulous care, Cubberley designed every cubic inch of the building and prescribed the furnishings. At the dedication in 1938 President Wilbur allowed that the building was "as comfortable as an old shoe."

Many of the basic characteristics of the School of Education today had their beginnings with Cubberley. When President Jordan's up-or-out deadline was safely passed, the education faculty in 1902 moved the department toward a more professional status. Until then any student who desired to teach had been accepted as a major. Thereafter, majors were required to become competent in a subject field as well as in the techniques of teaching. Greater emphasis was placed on training school administrators and on programs of research. The department clearly was headed toward graduate status, and Cubberley made sure his faculty choices were up to the job.

The appointment of Lewis M. Terman to the education faculty in 1910 was symbolic of the department's new direction. Terman and Edward L. Thorndike of Columbia's Teachers College are considered to be the founders of the field of educational psychology, and Terman began his famous, lifelong study of gifted children in 1921. Two years later he became head of the University's Psychology Department.

In 1917 the Education Department became the School of Education, with Cubberley as dean, and for the first time a secretary was employed to type the faculty's letters. In the same year Stanford shifted from a semester to a four-quarter system, an advantage for the school since many of its students were active teachers who could return during the summer for advanced work.

Although he received literally dozens of offers to go elsewhere at higher salaries, Cubberley elected to remain at Stanford. He retired in 1933, but the high standards he had set were not forgotten. They served the school well in the period after World War II when the number of schoolchildren multiplied dramatically, new laws and policies opened opportunities for minorities, the space race demanded immediate improvement in the teaching of mathematics and science, government intervention increased, and in many other ways education became more complex—all of which required a higher order of professionalism, research, and training for leadership.

Domestic challenges were matched by the massive effort needed to provide educational support for the economic and social advancement of developing nations. The Stanford School of Education was able to move quickly and surely in this direction because of the

Above: Card catalog in Cubberley Library. Right: CERAS.

presence on its faculty of Paul R. Hanna. Beginning in 1940 Hanna had participated in a series of overseas missions that included several educational projects in Latin America, counseling the commander of the European occupation on the reeducation of the German people, and service on a four-man international UNESCO team in the Philippines.

Professor Hanna realized that simply exporting U.S. methods of education to developing nations would not do, that country-by-country research was needed to understand the culture and determine appropriate educational strategies, after which both U.S. and foreign nationals could be trained to establish the new systems. The Stanford International Development Education Center, directed by Hanna and originally funded by the U.S. Office of Education and the Ford Foundation, was established in 1965 to carry out this dual function.

Today some 250 SIDEC alumni holding Stanford master's and doctoral degrees are presidents of universities, ministers of education, professors, members of U.S. government or foundation staffs overseas, or in other leading positions around the world. "They have done exceedingly well," comments Hanna, who is now retired from the education faculty and serves as a senior research fellow at the Hoover Institution.

A big step forward for the School of Education was the decision of 1954, when I. James Quillen became dean, that henceforth all faculty appointments would be made jointly by the School of Education and another academic discipline. Since then all candidates have been reviewed and appointments made by the discipline—English, sociology, anthropology, art, or whatever—and the School of Education together; rivalry and duplication have been replaced by cooperation.

Enrollment in the School of Education now runs to about 500 students, of whom half are working at the doctoral level and half at the master's level. (Undergraduate work was dropped entirely in the mid-sixties.) "We are turning out people who make a difference in the knowledge base," declares Arthur Coladarci, dean for the nine years ending in 1979 and a member of the faculty since 1952. (J. Myron Atkin, dean of the Illinois College of Education at Urbana, became the seventh dean of the school on September 1, 1979.) A majority of the school's doctoral holders become faculty members of schools of education or join the staffs of research organizations such as Educational Testing Service and the Rand Corporation, or they fill government posts.

The student body is culturally diverse. Twenty percent are minority students, compared to almost none ten years ago, and 20 percent are from abroad—principally Latin America and Asia, although the number from Europe and Africa is increasing. There are one black and three Chicano faculty members, and "we are not satisfied with these numbers; we keep searching for strong applicants," Coladarci states. He sees hope in the larger number of minority students among the school's doctoral candidates.

About $3 million is provided annually by federal and state agencies and private foundations for research into educational finance, instructional methods, measurement of the processes and outcomes of schooling, legal and political issues in the making of educational policy, and other areas. All members of the faculty are researchers as well as teachers. Much of the investigative work is done

Paul R. Hanna, Lee J. Jacks Professor of Child Education, emeritus, specialized in international and child education and was director of Stanford's International Development Education Center. Currently a senior research fellow at the Hoover Institution, he and his wife recently completed the manuscript for a book titled The Hannas' Honeycomb House *by Frank Lloyd Wright, an indepth study of the home Wright built for the Hannas on the Stanford campus.*

A view through a
CERAS skylight.

at the Center for Educational Research at Stanford, described by Coladarci as "a booming place." It is a large laboratory building constructed in 1972 with federal funds as part of a national network of educational research centers.

During the past decade the Stanford School of Education has been ranked consistently number one in the country. A 1977 poll of practicing scholars in education found the Stanford school so far in the lead in faculty quality and educational attractiveness that the pollsters referred to "Stanford's preeminent position." Educational attractiveness was defined as "the reputation and accessibility of faculty, curricula, innovative programs, library resources, other educational facilities, quality of students, prominence of alumni, and other factors which contribute to an effective and professional environment." A 1979 poll on faculty quality alone confirmed the Stanford school's top position.

"That kind of reputation, which I think our faculty has earned, attracts good students and strong new faculty members to us and bolsters our applications for research funding," Coladarci says. "It's a good idea to be on top."

Although he planned and paid for the entire Education Building (above), Dean Cubberley asked that only its library bear his name.

STOCKS, BONDS, AND BOOKS

For most of his adult life Ellwood P. Cubberley carried a pocket calendar book in which he made frequent entries about his professional life and such personal items as clothing expenses, illnesses, hotels patronized, and car repairs. (The books are now among his papers in the Stanford University Archives.) For May 18, 1911, he entered: "Made proposition to Houghton Mifflin company to publish a series of educational texts." Six days later he noted that Houghton Mifflin had agreed. This was the beginning of the Riverside Textbooks in Education.

Cubberley lined up leading educators to write the books; he then edited them and wrote the introductions. He continued as editor until his death in 1941, at which time 106 books had been published and a million and a half copies sold, with Cubberley's own books making up a quarter of the total.

His homespun records show that the Cubberleys kept their living expenses to the amount of his salary. Beginning with $400 in 1901, the dean invested in the stock market all the proceeds from his writing, lecturing, editing, and school survey work, basing his purchases on his study of materials in the Stanford library. The astuteness of his selections enabled him and Mrs. Cubberley to make gifts to the University that totaled $772,000.

The gifts were so large—especially for Depression years—and so unexpected that they were written up in 'Time,' and 'Barron's Weekly' assigned a writer to find the key to the dean's investing success. The key, he discovered, was simple enough: Buy stocks and bonds of good quality, have the nerve to stick with them, and compound.

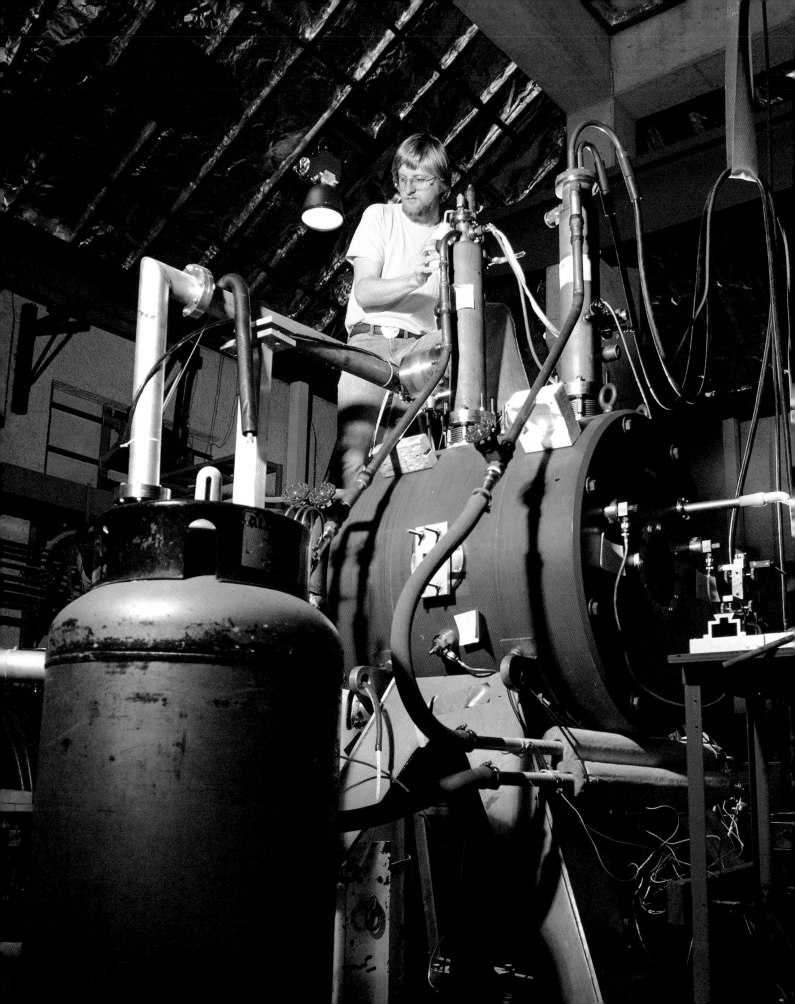

Engineering

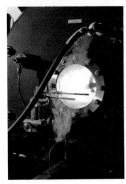

Fred Terman was in a mood for reminiscence. On the eve of retirement in 1965, the University provost was recalling his days as a young Stanford professor of electrical engineering during the Depression period of the thirties.

"The electronics laboratory was in an attic under the eaves," he related. "The roof of this attic leaked, and in time these leaks became quite bad. Whenever it rained, water would drip into the laboratory in numerous places!

"The University had no money to repair roofs; it met the situation by constructing big wooden trays which were lined with tar paper caulked with tar to make them watertight. These trays were then strategically deployed about the floor to catch the dripping water, and during the rainy season were always partially filled.

"One winter one of our more imaginative students, a likable fellow named Bill Hewlett, added a homelike touch to the laboratory by stocking these trays with goldfish, which he bought himself."

Another of Terman's promising students working in the attic lab was David Packard, and the future provost helped the two of them establish their own electronics company in a Palo Alto garage. In the years that followed Hewlett-Packard Company developed into a prosperous multinational electronics manufacturer. And the grateful partners, with their wives, provided the funds for construction in 1977 of the architecturally exciting and energy-efficient Frederick Emmons Terman Engineering Center. The Terman Center stands at the apex of the several buildings which were raised over the years to augment the lab with the porous roof and other early-day engineering facilities.

Charles D. Marx (above), an original faculty member in engineering, was an environmentalist long before the word entered the language. He would be pleased with Stanford's modern-day High Temperature Gasdynamics Laboratory, headed by Robert H. Eustis. The lab's 45 engineers are seeking ways to use existing fuels more efficiently and to cut down air pollution from power plants. The equipment shown above and on the facing page is for experiments in magnetohydrodynamics, a method for potentially wringing up to 50 percent more energy from coal.

When Leland and Jane Stanford were planning the University, one of the first ideas the Senator expressed was to "start a school for civil and mechanical engineering on my grounds in Palo Alto." Later they enlarged their concept to a full-scale university, but engineering—reflecting the western location and the Stanfords' desire to train students for "personal success and direct usefulness in life"—remained a prominent part. Two of the original 15 faculty members were engineers. They headed departments in civil and mechanical engineering. Electrical engineering,

with added personnel, was begun in the second year.

Some of the engineering laboratory buildings that now cluster south of the Quad were available when the University opened in 1891 and others were soon constructed. Engineering Corner, one of the principal buildings of the Outer Quad, was opened in 1905.

A spacious office on the second floor of Engineering Corner, its curved windows overlooking the busiest crossroad of foot traffic on the campus, was occupied for years by Charles David Marx, the first civil engineer on the faculty. The mustachioed and bearded professor became known as "Daddy" Marx to the generations of students who were inspired by his teaching. It was he who laid down philos-

ophies which still guide the work in engineering at Stanford.

Again and again Marx emphasized two goals: that the engineer must be broadly educated in language, social science, and writing as well as in technical subjects, and that the engineer's vision must extend beyond narrow professionalism to the needs of the whole society. The two, of course, are interleaved.

"We do not admit," Marx told his students, "...that the higher wants of man have no rights on the premises." He challenged them to bring "structures into harmony with their surroundings" and to strive for "the pure air, the pure earth, the pure water," and for "freeing men from soul- and mind-killing drudgery."

Although the School of Engineering moved out of Engineering Corner when the Terman Center was completed in 1977, it is not likely the name of this landmark intersection will ever disappear from the Stanford glossary.

William Frederick Durand, another early-day Stanford professor of engineering, exhorted engineers to "seek out the mountaintops, . . . to place ourselves in relation to the great problems and movements of the day." He told them: "Life is like some intricately woven web of chain mail wherein each link is necessary to, and in turn dependent upon, all the others."

And William M. Kays, who was appointed fifth dean of the School of Engineering in 1972, has observed, "Stanford is one of the few universities in the world where a very highly regarded engineering school is integrated into a strong environment of humanists and social scientists. There is a unique opportunity here to produce the kind of socially conscious and sensitive engineer that is now needed."

From its beginning Stanford posted the same high standards for engineering courses as it did for all others, wiping out the line that divided technical from cultural study in most other institutions. Professor Marx recalled that the University "took the stand that all studies, if pursued in the proper spirit under the direction of able and inspiring teachers, are of equal cultural value."

In 1925 the School of Engineering was formed, putting an end to the rugged independence of the four separate departments. Theodore J. Hoover, head of the Mining Department, was the first dean. The leadership of the school, abetted by President Wilbur, put new emphasis on graduate study and freed the undergraduate for more nonprofessional courses. "If the engineering school is to turn out leaders," reported a study committee, "it must first catch them and, having caught them, should have a care that the course of instruction calls forth

Above: Early engineering students learned mechanics and the properties of metals in this forge and lathe shop. The same building, after a series of tenants, was recently remodeled for the High Temperature Gasdynamics Laboratory. Left: Automotive engineering was a major interest before World War II.

Above: Frederick Emmons Terman, master builder of the Stanford School of Engineering.

"The Terman Engineering Center—this anti-technocratic work of art is an engineering building—has adjustable wooden shutters that can be pushed aside in winter to let the sun in, or drawn in summer to keep the interiors shadowy and cool, setting up a seasonal architectonic rhythm on the relaxed but elegant facades.

"Moreover, the building is ventilated by fresh air, blowing through open windows, and upward through corridors, stairs, and air-wells to open skylights in the roof, rather than by air conditioning behind sealed glass in a structure crammed with costly mechanical apparatus.

"There are no windowless interior compounds. Instead, secretaries, students, research assistants, and professors can look up from work, out over trees and grass, to distant hills. These are only a few of the many acts of courtesy in a building that everywhere displays exquisite consideration for the people who actually use it. . . .

"It all comes together as a triumph of common sense."

—Allan Temko
Architecture Critic
San Francisco Chronicle

Top: An Engineering Design Division class meets in the Terman Center. Inside the domed Imaginarium music, films, slides, sound effects, and smells conspire to enhance the occupant's creative powers.

rather than represses the exercise of initiative and judgment on the part of the student."

Today this attitude is given specific expression at the undergraduate level in the engineering-inspired but multidisciplinary program called Values, Technology, and Society. "We have to discuss the questions which confront the students as citizens and voters," states a VTS founder, mechanical engineering professor Stephen J. Kline. "What will they need to know about health care, nuclear power, genetic control, or data banks? This is the kind of question we should worry about, just as 50 years ago we should have worried about the effect of the auto on the inner city."

The School of Engineering emerged from World War II in a weakened state. It had acquired some elements of national visibility, but it had not been in a strong enough posi-

FROM JIBS TO JETS

William Frederick Durand, a gentle genius in a rugged profession, began his engineering career in sailing ships and ended it as a pioneer in the design of jet aircraft.

Fresh out of Annapolis in 1880, he was assigned to the U.S.S. 'Tennessee,' flagship of the North Atlantic fleet. She was wood-hulled and full-rigged, but Durand's job was to look after the steam engines that took over when the wind failed. He left the navy in 1887 for the academic world, and his research at Cornell eliminated the guesswork from the design of marine screw propellers.

After coming to Stanford in 1904 Durand applied his background in fluid mechanics to the water and power problems of the Western states. But with the development of the airplane his old love of propellers returned, and his long series of experiments in a Stanford wind tunnel became the authoritative source for their design.

During World War I Durand—a slightly built, bearded scholar—played a leading part in the development of military aircraft. In 1917 he was one of the first three engineers elected to the National Academy of Sciences.

Durand returned to Stanford shortly after the armistice and reached retirement age in 1924. Thereupon began a remarkable sequence of service on high government commissions—among them studies of the integration of aircraft in national defense (after the Gen. Billy Mitchell scandal), feasibility of the Hoover Dam, and fish ladders for the Grand Coulee Dam. But most remarkable of all was his call to Washington in 1941, when he was 82, to head the development of jet propulsion for application to aircraft. The first U.S. jet plane was test-flown late in 1942.

Durand died in Brooklyn, where he had gone to be near his son, in 1958 at the age of 99. In 1969 Stanford dedicated the William Frederick Durand Building for Space Engineering and Science—its memorial to this remarkable engineer.

tion to participate in the exciting technical developments generated by the war. All of this was changed by Terman, who returned to Stanford to become dean of the school after directing the wartime Radio Research Laboratory at Harvard, which successfully developed radar countermeasures.

Terman was in a position to see how the "bank" of basic engineering knowledge had been depleted during the war as researchers devoted their time and talents almost exclusively to the tremendous demands for sophisticated weapons, aircraft, detection devices, and other war-related applications. He surmised correctly that, with the return of peace, graduate study in engineering would assume new importance and that for the first time large amounts of money would be available to support engineering research. The plan which he devised, and which started Stanford on a steady climb into the front rank of engineering schools, was simple and direct: government-sponsored research would be a part of the educational process; it would

Antennae for iono-spheric and planetary exploration, operated by the Radioscience Laboratory, are scattered over 2,000 campus foothill acres. This is the "Big Dish," used to make man's first radar contact with the sun in 1960.

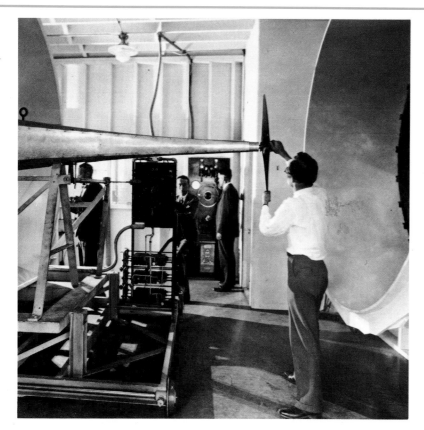

be performed by students and faculty together; and only projects having substantial academic value would be undertaken.

The concept that Terman developed and labeled "steeples of excellence" steered the school away from trying to be merely good at everything. Rather, the school concentrated faculty and resources on a limited number of important areas and built the highest possible quality into each.

Terman also perceived that there was a community of interest between the University and local industry, especially in engineering. In 1974 *Fortune* magazine called the buildup of 800 pioneering technology companies along the San Francisco Peninsula "almost wholly the handiwork of Frederick Terman."

The academic world woke up to what was

happening in the Stanford School of Engineering when the National Science Foundation began its Graduate Fellowship Program in 1952. Fellowship winners were free to pick their place of study and only M.I.T. outranked Stanford as the choice of engineers. Since that time graduate enrollment has shown explosive growth. There were 258 advanced students in 1952, 1,820 in 1979. Undergraduate enrollment, reflecting changes in student interests, declined through the sixties but more than doubled in the seventies to reach 1,048 in 1979. A quarter of the 1979 undergraduates were women, making engineering, for the first time, one of the most popular majors for women. Dean Kays attributed this in part to the discovery that engineering is a "virtually untapped field" for women with mathematical talent.

Above, left: The wind tunnel of the Daniel Guggenheim Aeronautics Laboratory, capable of whipping up an air velocity of 90 miles an hour. This was where Professors William F. Durand and Everett P. Lesley conducted pioneering studies of airplane propellers before World War I. Above, right: Creativity and practicality are linked by the Design Division of Mechanical Engineering. In the "Design Loft," students often devise whimsical solutions to practical problems.

Above: The Engineering Library in the new Terman Center. Left: A chemical engineering graduate student in the Bioengineering Laboratory tests the properties of artificial ultrafiltration membranes. Among their uses is the preparation of pharmaceuticals.

George B. Dantzig, professor of operations research and of computer science, was awarded the National Medal of Science in 1976 for inventing linear programming and discovering methods that led to more efficient use of mathematical theory in computers. He is the coauthor of Compact City, *a book that describes a new concept of living in which as many as two million people could live in comfortable and attractive surroundings within a few minutes of their jobs.*

About 300 students a year participate in the Honors Cooperative Program, which was begun in 1955. They are employees of some 50 companies in the San Francisco Bay Area who are granted time off with pay to take engineering courses leading to a degree, and most of them do their classwork without ever leaving the company premises. This is made possible by the Stanford Instructional Television Network, which transmits classes live from an array of antennae on Black Mountain behind the campus to receiving facilities provided by the participating companies. In most cases the remote students participate in

In the Laboratory for the Study of Adsorption and Catalysis in the Chemical Engineering Department, a graduate student checks the action of molybdenum as a catalyst in the synthesis of ammonia.

classroom discussion via a two-way audio linkup.

From a negligible amount—possibly $10,000—in the pre-World War II period, engineering research at Stanford now runs about $25 million a year, involving some 200 grants and contracts. The range is universal, from microscopic integrated circuits to all of outer space. Stanford engineers are researching at the forefront of urban planning, energy conservation, satellite communication, system analysis, mathematical modeling in decision making, medical electronics, radio astronomy, spacecraft design, production management, the internal structure of materials, and other fields. To a significant degree they join forces with researchers in other schools of the University.

For 30 years electronics has been the largest element of the school's research program. "This is fortunate," Dean Kays has pointed out, "because it is apparent we are about 50 years into an electronics revolution that is going to affect society as much as did the 200-year-old Industrial Revolution. The Industrial Revolution was *energy and material intensive* and had the effect of extending the physical capabilities of man through harnessing large amounts of mechanical energy. The electronics revolution is *information intensive* and its principal thrust is the extension of the intellectual capabilities of man through processing large amounts of information electronically."

As the School of Engineering takes part in this new revolution, probably the most exciting and important technical development of the century, the appeal sounded so long ago by Marx and Durand to look from the mountaintops continues to be sound advice.

The Hugh Hildreth Skilling Building, named for a longtime favorite professor of electrical engineering, contains a small auditorium and classrooms equipped for instruction by closed-circuit television.

MECHANICAL ENGINEERING

The Graduate School of Business building from the Hoover Tower observation platform.

Business

When Arjay Miller, then vice-chairman and former president of Ford Motor Co., was approached about becoming dean of the Graduate School of Business in 1968, he agreed—with one condition. He wanted a free hand to expand the school's traditional job of training managers for private business to include the same training for managers in government. Based on his firsthand experience, Miller felt that the "tools and concepts that are successful in the private sector can be successful in the public sector."

As president of Ford, Miller had watched the Detroit ghetto riots of 1967 and then had taken the lead among businessmen who helped to rebuild the city. He also became founding chairman of the Urban Institute, a national organization studying the social ills of cities. The real need, he perceived from these activities, was to pump more managerial talent into government staffs.

As it turned out, Miller's condition was readily granted because a faculty long-range

Members of the Business School's Class of '29 pose on graduation day.

planning committee had already been thinking along the same lines, and George L. Bach, dean of the business school of Carnegie-Mellon, had been recruited to the Stanford faculty in 1966 with this mission in mind. Miller accepted the deanship and came to Stanford in 1969. The Public Management Program got under way in 1971 and the following year Henry S. Rowen, onetime assistant director of the Bureau of the Budget and later president of the Rand Corporation, became its director. The program turned out 283 graduates in its first eight years and most of them joined government or nonprofit organizations.

The Business School traces its beginning to an encampment in the California redwoods in 1924 when Herbert Hoover, then secretary of commerce in the Coolidge cabinet, proposed to a group of friends that a school be established at Stanford to "teach business as a profession upon a parity with engineering, law, and medicine."

"The induction of professional ideals, professional standing, and professional skill into the largest of our occupations is a primary necessity," Hoover continued in a follow-up memorandum. He pointed out that California youths were going East to attend business schools and then remaining there to pursue their careers. "California is losing many good brains," he said.

Hoover's friends assembled 125 Pacific Coast business leaders in September of 1924 and they agreed to raise the funds. At the Stanford commencement in June 1925, President Wilbur announced that the Graduate School of Business would open in the fall—barely more than a year from the time of the meeting in the redwoods.

The school's first dean, Willard E. Hotch-

kiss, who had organized business schools at the University of Minnesota and Northwestern University, arrived in July and in less than two months was ready for the first class of 16. They took up their work in borrowed space in Jordan Hall, the biology building, where the fragrance of pickled dogfish permeated the halls.

The Graduate School of Business building (above) was completed and dedicated in October 1966. The dean's office looks out into the branches of the huge Class of '95 oak (right).

Two of the first three faculty appointees were Eliot G. Mears, a noted geographer and expert in international trade, and Edward K. Strong, known in this country and abroad for his work in vocational testing. They were joined in the second year by economist George W. Dowrie, who left the deanship of the business school at the University of Minnesota; Paul E. Holden, management expert from the staff of the U.S. Chamber of Commerce; and J. Hugh Jackson, a practicing CPA and Harvard professor. These five were the vanguard of a considerable company who served out distinguished careers as members of the Business School faculty.

Professor Jackson began a 26-year occupancy of the dean's chair in 1932. The Great Depression was at its nadir and he saw the times as a challenge to produce graduates with "a keen sense of social responsibility"

and to make "a maximum contribution toward the supremacy of competence and morality in the business world."

Although outwardly an austere and nononsense administrator, Jackson was acutely sensitive to human values. An alumnus of the class of '35, the year the unemployment rate rose to 18 percent, returned to the school to tell the dean that he had landed his first job at $1,500 a year. "He asked me to hold on and went into his office," the graduate recalls. "When he came out he told me he had negotiated with my boss for an additional $300 a year." A new, young faculty member and his wife remember the dean's driving them around to look for a place to live and holding their baby on his lap while they inspected various homes.

Soon after the old Assembly Hall on the Outer Quad was remodeled into a two-story

The Flamebirds *sculpture by François Stahly, an artist-in-residence in the 1960s, has enhanced the Business School patio since the building's dedication. The patio and base of the sculpture were designed by Thomas Church, often called the "father of landscape architecture."*

home for the school in 1937, enrollment surged beyond 200. A survey showed that 79 percent of the alumni lived on the Pacific Coast. Following the post-World War II boom, enrollment settled at 400.

The school's highly regarded group of advanced management programs was launched in 1952 with the Executive Development Program—eight summer weeks in residency, with classes six hours a day, five days a week. Now renamed the Stanford Executive Program, it attracts 185 senior-level executives each year from throughout the world. Under the impetus of Acting Dean Carlton A. Pederson and with the backing of the Sloan Foundation, the Stanford Sloan Program was begun in 1957. Still going strong, it brings to the Business School for nine months of study 42 middle managers who have the potential for early entry into senior management. A half dozen other advanced programs of shorter duration are offered, including one conducted in France for Europeans and overseas managers of U.S. firms.

In 1958 Ernest C. Arbuckle, Stanford '33, M.B.A. '36, left his post as executive vice-president of W.R. Grace and Co. to become the Business School's third dean. He was persuaded "to come home, but not to roost"— in the phrase of the *Alumni Bulletin*—and in his ten years as dean he used his management skills to move the school energetically forward.

Outstanding new professors were recruited throughout the country and the number of faculty grew from 29 to 76. By design, student enrollment was held to an increase from 400 to 550, but the quality and number of applicants was improved dramatically by new recruiting methods. "Our young students are so good, they push you to the wall with questions," commented an associate dean.

The earlier regional character of the student body all but disappeared. The faculty debated, drafted, and put into effect a strengthened curriculum, and the amount of faculty research was stepped up markedly. Arbuckle did not, however, allow the school to swerve from its traditional emphasis on preparing students for high-level careers in general management.

Annual seminars on business ethics, held at Asilomar on Monterey Bay and attended by second-year M.B.A. students and business leaders, were begun in 1965. An offshoot of the seminars is the Committee for Corporate Responsibility, a voluntary student organization which brings together students and business executives to debate social issues confronting business. The Stanford group sparked the formation of similar programs in other business schools and eventually a national organization.

In 1966 the school moved into a brand-new home, a three-story complex of classrooms, offices, library, and auditorium. Arbuckle called it "a symbol of the coming of age of education for business administration in competition with the older professional schools of medicine, law, and engineering." He was careful to locate the dean's office so that its windows look out into the branches of the huge class of '95 oak, a campus landmark familiar to him from his student days.

Arbuckle left the dean's chair in 1968 to become board chairman of Wells Fargo Bank, and the following year began the Miller decade. In addition to installing the Public Management Program, Miller infused the curriculum with new courses, particularly in the areas of consumerism and environmentalism, decision making, and the human aspects of business management.

An exponent of corporate responsibility as both civic duty and good business policy, George Leland "Lee" Bach is Frank E. Buck Professor of Economics and Public Policy and also has an appointment in the Department of Economics. Best known for his books on basic economics, the Federal Reserve, inflation, monetary policy, and mangement education, Bach received the first Dow Jones Award for Distinguished Contributions to Management Education in 1976.

A DEAN FOR ALL SEASONS

If there is a more "compleat Stanfordite" than Ernest C. (Ernie) Arbuckle—undergraduate and graduate student, student body officeholder, assistant to the dean of men, manager of his fraternity, Block "S" winner, Stanford Associates executive committee member, professor and dean, member of the Board of Trustees—he or she would be hard to find.

Ernie didn't win his varsity letter in the usual way. As junior manager of the track team he was detailed during practice to shag the javelins and toss them back to the varsity throwers. The coach, Dink Templeton, noticed that Ernie was getting more distance than the experts and put him on the team. In his remaining full season as a senior he won his Block "S."

After receiving the M.B.A. in 1936, Arbuckle lined up a job with Standard Oil Company of California. On the Friday before the Monday he was to report, a friend whose father had willed him the money to travel around the world asked Ernie to go along. "The people at Standard said to go ahead," Arbuckle recalls. "When we returned 15 months later, Standard paid me $150 a month, $25 more than I was originally offered."

Arbuckle, commissioned a Navy ensign in April 1941, volunteered for torpedo boat duty. Off the north coast of Sicily the PT boat under his command was outgunned and badly damaged in a sea battle. Ernie, seriously injured, propped himself up in a corner of the chart house and pulled the crew together. Hours later they made it back to Palermo Harbor. Ernie was awarded the Silver Star.

Arbuckle returned to the executive corridors of San Francisco and stayed until 1958. Then he

Dean Arbuckle, winner of the "Red Hot Professor" title in a penny-a-vote-for-charity contest among students, gets to lead the Axe Yell at the 1967 football game with Oregon.

heeded the urgings of Stanford's President Sterling and some of his friends to accept appointment as dean of the Graduate School of Business. The president had known Ernie as a Stanford trustee but doubtless his memory also harked back to the time in 1935 when Ernie was pitching for the Business School's intramural softball team and one of his toughest outs was a husky graduate student in history named Wally Sterling.

faculty it was time for him "to repot." Rene C. McPherson, chairman and chief executive officer of Dana Corporation, was named his successor, effective September 1, 1980. In addition to directing the Toledo, Ohio, motor vehicle parts manufacturing firm with annual sales exceeding $2 billion, McPherson has been very active in support of higher education as an adviser and executive-in-residence.

In 1975, the school's fiftieth anniversary year, an academic poll for the first time boosted the Stanford Business School from its usual second or third position to first in the nation. Since then several other polls have confirmed this rating. Said Miller at the time of his resignation: "I'm thoroughly convinced Stanford has the best business school and am confident it has the people to keep it that way."

In Miller's era the first women were appointed to the faculty. The total faculty grew from 76 to 84, while endowed chairs rose from 6 to 21. Although applications for the M.B.A. program rose sharply, from 1,700 to 4,200 annually, enrollment was held to a modest gain, from 550 to 600. The number of black students jumped from 5 to 26, Spanish-surnamed from none to 24, Asian-Americans from 4 to 27, and women from 10 to 146.

For a man who once described himself as "just an old bookkeeper," Miller made remarkable changes in the school's financial position. Endowment rose from $6.4 million to $23.2 million, pledges receivable from less than $50,000 to more than $5 million, income from business affiliates from $300,000 annually to more than $1.3 million, and annual alumni giving from $130,000 to $600,000. No wonder he often counseled students that finance is a good route to the top of a business organization.

Arjay Miller chose to resign in 1979, borrowing from the gardening lexicon to tell his

Above, left: Students lunch on the patio of the Business School with Memorial Hall as a backdrop. Left: Arjay Miller had just completed five years as president of Ford Motor Co. when he became dean of the Stanford Business School. His conviction that business schools should train managers for government and education as well as business was well received by both faculty and students, and during his tenure Stanford's business education program became ranked first in the nation. He is shown at his final Commencement in June 1979.

Law

"Stanford University, where the winds of freedom still circulate through pleasant quadrangles, old and new, was built and still stands upon that solid triad of law, learning, and liberty."

Gerald R. Ford, president of the United States, was speaking to the throng of 10,000 people who had gathered for the dedication in 1975 of Crown Quadrangle, the fine and functional new home of the Stanford Law School.

"The commitment of Americans to law, learning, and liberty continues in this very court this afternoon," he went on to say

"But contradictions and dilemmas remain in our society in abundance. They will always exist in a democratic nation where the delicate balances between freedom and order, between private right and public interest, between the safety of the state and the security of the individual, all require constant review and resolution."

President Ford was speaking on the grounds of an institution singularly well prepared to strike the "delicate balance" to which he referred. The Stanford Law School has built a reputation for excellence in teaching and research by following the principle that small is better. With a student body of 500 and a faculty of 35 to 40, the school has been able to be highly selective in both instances and to provide for close interaction between pupil and mentor.

"It is a rich life, constantly renewed by inquiring young people, by productive associations on campus and off, and by the wellsprings of imagination that we may be lucky enough to have within ourselves," observes Dean Charles J. Meyers.

Established in 1893, just as legal education was being revolutionized by the introduction

The Benjamin Scott Crocker Garden in the center of the Law School quadrangle offers moments of respite from the demanding pace of law classes.

of Socratic exchange and casebooks in place of abstract lectures and treatises, the Stanford Law School today is in the midst of another revolution. This time the information base and the skills of students are being substantially broadened so that, as practicing lawyers, they will be flexible enough to cope with the shifts and expansions in the law which arise from social and technological change.

This is being done at Stanford in two principal ways—by the integration of other academic disciplines of the University into the law curriculum and by the introduction of the clinical teaching method.

"Law is not a self-contained discipline," Dean Meyers says. "You cannot understand natural resources law or antitrust law without understanding economics. You cannot understand administrative law without knowing the political system, constitutional law without knowing history, and so on."

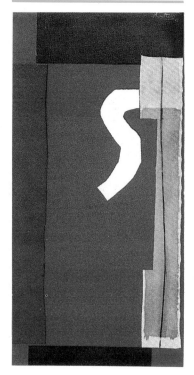

Right: The spacious vestibule of the four-story Robert Crown Library. Encircling the library on each floor are offices of faculty, administration, and student organizations. Semiprivate carrels for 350 students are located in the open stacks. Above: In Celebration was the name given by the distinguished artist, Robert Motherwell, Stanford '37, to his oil and collage that honored the opening of the Law School quadrangle. It was commissioned by Richard Lang, a 1929 graduate of the school.

Gerald Gunther, William Nelson Cromwell Professor of Law, is a foremost authority on constitutional law; his casebooks on this subject are the most widely used in American law schools. Recognized as an excellent teacher, Gunther has written widely on contemporary and historical problems of constitutional law. His current projects are a biography of Judge Learned Hand, for whom he clerked, and a history of the Supreme Court at the time of Chief Justice John Marshall.

Law students are encouraged to take supplementary courses in other schools of the University, and joint-degree programs are available with business, history, economics, and political science. Several law professors hold joint appointments and professors from other departments give courses in the Law School.

In clinical teaching a group of 10 or 12 students and their professor handle a simulated legal problem from beginning to end. Originally used to teach the skill of conducting trials, the method has now been expanded to real estate transactions, settlement conferences, contract negotiations, and client negotiations. Students must deal with client, judge, jury, and coworker under the same pressures of time and personality that exist in life. These simulations can become remarkably real to students as they live with the responsibilities they have accepted. Their performances are videotaped, then extensively analyzed during critique sessions.

"The clinical method makes students do the job of the lawyer," Dean Meyers comments. "And, most importantly, they are learning what is very difficult to teach, the exercise of lawyer judgment."

He predicts that use of the clinical method will grow but that it will not supplant the case method as the basic tool of first-year instruction. The study of judicial opinions, sharpened by the probing questions of the teacher, is still the better way for developing analytic ability.

Another way for students to gain insights into the actual practice of law is afforded by the school's decade-old extern program. Selected students spend either their fourth or fifth semester away from the school in a variety of assignments: as clerks to trial court and appellate judges, in work-study assignments at public interest law firms like the Center for Law and Social Policy in Washington, D.C., assisting in the Washington offices of U.S. senators, working with probation officers, or assisting in three comparative law institutes abroad.

Associate Dean Joseph E. Leininger describes the externs as being deeply involved. "With guidance, they are thrown into the mill of the office to which they are assigned," he notes. "They're not doing donkey work."

In addition to carrying a full teaching load, all Stanford law professors are engaged in independent research, and here again the multidisciplinary trend is strong. Research has expanded beyond traditional professional limits to be concerned with the effects of law and justice on the behavior of people, and how legal systems mesh with social, economic, and political systems: Barbara Babcock is studying sex discrimination and the law; Michael Wald, juvenile delinquency; Victor Li, law and politics in China's foreign trade; William Gould, racial discrimination in labor relations; John Kaplan, drug controls; Charles Meyers, water resources policy; and Byron Sher, consumer protection, to give some examples.

Demanding though the formal course work may be, a majority—perhaps all—of the students are involved in at least one of the more than 20 extracurricular organizations.

The Environmental Law Society, one of the most active of the student groups, sponsors summertime research and fieldwork in such areas as legal incentives and barriers to solar energy, the initiative process, the powers of land-use agencies, urban sprawl, historic preservation, and protection of desert lands. The results are made available to the pub-

lic in a series of practical, citizen-oriented booklets.

The traditional Legal Aid Society provides good practice and makes urgently needed legal assistance available to the poor in communities near Stanford. Often an indigent person who would refuse to go to a lawyer's office will unburden himself to a student working in the community. The students also assist local leaders in broader attacks on social problems.

Organization work can sharpen professional skills. The *Stanford Law Review* and the *Stanford Journal of International Studies* demand analytic and writing abilities. Courtroom techniques are developed by participants in the Moot Court Board and Serjeants at Law, which takes its name from a select circle of English barristers.

"Several organizations give students who are up to their necks in studies a way to be-come politically involved," LaDoris Hazzard Cordell, assistant dean for student affairs and a recent alumna of the school, comments. "They are made aware of the outside world. They gain a different focus."

The Stanford Law School typically receives about 3,500 applications for the 167 places in each entering class. So the competition is fierce, and the school ends up drawing its student body from the top 3 percent of those who enter law schools each year. At the other end of the line, representatives from about 500 firms and agencies come to the school to interview members of the graduating class about jobs.

The numbers and pressures were considerably smaller when law was first offered at Stanford in 1893, the University's third year. Forty-six students—3 graduate, 35 undergraduate, and 8 special—registered in the first class. The faculty consisted of a former

The oak-paneled moot court room.

Anthony G. Amsterdam, holder of the Kenneth and Harle Montgomery Professorship in Clinical and Legal Education, is one of the nation's leading experts in criminal law and civil rights.

Alexander Calder's stabile, Le Faucon, *in the Arthur E. Cooley Courtyard.*

Marion Rice Kirkwood headed the Stanford School of Law for 22 years (1922-45), longer than any other dean in the school's history. An authority on property law, Kirkwood was Stanford educated (A.B. '09, J.D. '11) and was appointed to the law faculty by David Starr Jordan in 1912. At the time of his retirement in 1952, all but 80 of the Law School's graduates had received a substantial part of their legal education in his classroom. The Marion Rice Kirkwood Professorship in Law, established in his honor in 1952, is currently held by Lawrence M. Friedman. Kirkwood died in 1978 at the age of 90.

president of the United States, Benjamin Harrison, and the University librarian, Edward Hamlin Woodruff, who was pressed into service because he held a Cornell law degree. The following year Nathan Abbott arrived from Northwestern University's law faculty to head the department and he soon installed a normal curriculum with adequate faculty. In 1908 the department was changed to the School of Law.

Full professional status was attained in 1924 when Stanford joined Harvard and Pennsylvania as the only law schools requiring an A.B. degree for admission. This step up occurred early in the tenure of Dean Marion Rice Kirkwood, whose career in the Law School spanned 40 years. He had obtained an A.B. in economics at Stanford in 1909 and the J.D. in 1911. After a year of teaching at the University of Oklahoma, he was recalled by President Jordan to be assistant professor of law. He served as dean from 1922 to 1945 and retired from teaching in 1952. He died on January 8, 1978, at the

age of 90, the last surviving faculty member to have been appointed by Dr. Jordan.

Continuity and change have been the lot of the Law School. This was the burden of Charles Meyers's first message to alumni and friends of the school after he became dean in 1975. "In only 14 years, the time I've been teaching here, major changes have occurred in the faculty, the library, and the physical plant," he wrote. "There have been other changes as well, notably in curriculum, in the increased number of applications for admission, and (a Dean is obliged to say) in the cost of doing business.

"But these changes have occurred, have been *accomplished* is a word that better describes the process, with conscious concern for continuity with the past and with specific attention to the continuing and central goal of the school: The education and training of men and women to excel in the practice of law. That has always been the aim of the school and I trust that it will always continue to be."

John Kaplan, Jackson Eli Reynolds Professor of Law, is an expert in the field of drug control and the author of Marijuana—The New Prohibition. *Outside of his law school classes, he has lectured in several departments and schools at Stanford and offers an extraordinarily popular undergraduate course,* The Criminal Law and the Criminal System.

ARCHITECTURE AND ACADEMICS

The Stanford Law School has lived in Crown Quadrangle since the fall of 1975, and experience has proven it to be one of those facilities that enhances the academic process. This was not a lucky accident.

Before the architect set pencil to drawing paper—even before an architect was chosen—a group of faculty sat down with members of the University's Planning Office staff to determine just what a Stanford Law School facility should and should not be. Over a period of months they produced a building program which Professor John Henry Merryman, their chairman, says was "as big as a Sears Roebuck catalog."

"Our principal objective was to design the buildings for maximum student-faculty interaction, and we carried this right down to the traffic pattern," Merryman explains.

Space that was too small and poorly arranged had been a cross borne by the Law School for most of its life. After spending 57 years in small Inner Quad buildings, the school moved in 1950 to the remodeled Administration Building on the Outer Quad. As the student body and library continued to grow, the need for more room soon became acute again. In 1965 the ten-year process of fund raising, planning, and construction began.

Four buildings make up Crown Quadrangle. The largest is Robert Crown Library, which

shelves 250,000 volumes and has room for 250,000 more. The building also contains offices for faculty and administration, rooms for student organizations, and an individual work place for every student, usually a carrel in the library.

Opposite the library building is F.I.R. Hall (donated by Frederick I. Richman), which contains six classrooms, seven seminar and conference rooms, and the moot court room. Immediately adjoining the classrooms are small "after class" rooms where students and professors can continue discussions without interruption by the next class session.

The two main buildings are connected by the James Irvine Gallery, a "main street" from which meeting rooms and lounges open. The fourth building is Kresge Auditorium, with seats for 580, enough to hold the total population of the school. In the courtyard between these two buildings is the Benjamin Scott Crocker Garden, a sunny place where students and faculty gather informally.

The Arthur E. Cooley Courtyard forms the main entrance to Crown Quadrangle. Its center-piece is the late Alexander Calder's heroic stabile, 'Le Faucon' (The Falcon). The three-ton sculpture, a gift of Mr. and Mrs. Richard Lang of Seattle, was for many years the frontispiece of Calder's studio in Sache, France.

Medicine

Most of the people under 65 who die of heart disease in the United States could be saved if they would change their life-styles, but very few manage to do so.

"For 25 years medical science has known the risk factors that lead to coronary disease, but if you cannot make people stop smoking or change their diets, this knowledge is useless," Dr. John W. Farquhar, a Stanford Medical School professor, has declared.

Now, however, Dr. Farquhar and Nathan Maccoby, director of Stanford's Institute for Communication Research, are on the trail of a solution. They believe that organized community-based efforts can succeed where uncoordinated national campaigns, books, and magazine articles have failed. In a recently completed test in two small California communities, they distributed heart disease information intensively by radio, television, newspapers, billboards, and printed material. The media barrage was coordinated with instruction at local small-group meetings involving 600 high-risk individuals. The result was a 25 percent reduction in the communities' estimated risk of heart attack and stroke. The method is now being extended to larger cities in a new five-year program.

Maccoby, Farquhar, and their associates have shown that ingrained health habits can be changed. They have shown something else—that medical scientists and social scientists could do something together which they could not do separately. The project grew from a casual exchange of ideas between the two investigators, yet their paths probably never would have crossed had it not been for Stanford's bold decision in the mid-fifties to pick up its Medical School bodily and move it from San Francisco to the main campus near Palo Alto. Said President Sterling at

the time, "The future progress of the medical sciences is inextricably linked with progress in the basic physical and biological sciences and increasingly with progress in the social sciences." The benefits of the move have turned out to be even greater than expected, in teaching as well as in research.

Current research projects combining electronics and medicine include development of an ultrasonic imaging device enabling doctors to "see" into damaged eyes, an ultrasound device which detects the velocity of blood flowing through vessels by bouncing high-frequency waves off red blood cells, and telemetry systems so small they can be implanted in the body to study the response of the heart to drugs or to forms of stress.

Computer experts and anesthesiologists have developed a system for processing data during an operation. Physicists and radiologists, after pioneering the development of medical linear accelerators, continue to work

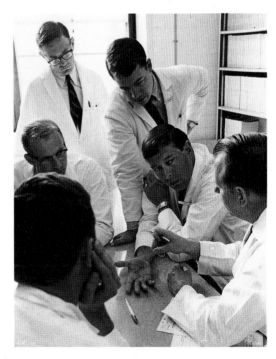

Robert A. Chase, (seated, lower right) Emile Holman Professor of Surgery, is particularly noted for his work in reconstructive surgery of the upper extremities. Head of the Department of Surgery from 1963 until 1974, he left Stanford to serve as president of the National Board of Medical Examiners for three years, returning in September of 1977. He is well known for his teaching and leadership in medical curriculum innovation, residency training, and continuing medical education.

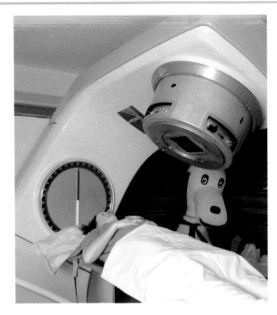

A HEALING BEAM

The medical linear accelerator designed and built in Stanford laboratories in the early fifties—the first practical megavoltage X-ray machine for the treatment of cancer patients—has been placed on display at the Smithsonian Institution's Museum of History and Technology.

The idea for building the pioneering machine was Dr. Henry Kaplan's. Then head of the Department of Radiology at the Stanford School of Medicine, he proposed a collaboration to Stanford physicists, who had achieved world leadership in the development of electron linear accelerators, a type of atom smasher.

It was known that megavoltage devices (those with a beam utilizing more than a million electron volts) were superior to conventional, lower-voltage X-ray machines for cancer therapy. They could penetrate tissue more deeply, were more destructive of cancer cells, and did relatively little damage to surrounding healthy tissue. But they could not be moved and aimed at different parts of the body, and they were far too expensive to be in general use.

The Stanford team overcame these problems. Kaplan provided the medical specifications and Edward L. Ginzton, then head of the University's Microwave Laboratory, did much of the design and supervised construction.

The first patient, a two-year-old boy who had already lost one eye to cancer and was threatened with blindness because of tumors on the retina of the other, was treated initially on January 30, 1956. The penetrating beam of the electron accelerator, over the course of 38 treatments, destroyed the tumors and saved the child's eyesight. Sixteen years and 8,000 patients later the machine was donated to the Smithsonian. In the meantime, more sophisticated models based on the Stanford design had been placed in operation at the Stanford Medical Center and in hospitals around the world.

Dr. Kaplan, internationally known for his progress in the fight against cancer, is Maureen Lyles D'Ambrogio Professor of Radiology and director of the Louis B. Mayer Cancer Biology Research Laboratory at the Stanford School of Medicine. In 1979 he was one of three cowinners of the first Charles F. Kettering Prize from the General Motors Cancer Research Foundation. Each winner received a gold medal and $100,000.

together on more sophisticated versions of atom smashers that destroy cancer cells while sparing surrounding tissue.

Professors in the Economics Department and the Graduate School of Business who have joint appointments in the Medical School are researching health care delivery systems and the effects on medical practice of the supply of doctors and fee structures. Professors in the School of Education, joining with those in medicine and communication, are working on youth and adult group health education in the latest heart disease prevention program.

In the teaching area the crossovers that have developed between Medical School faculty and the rest of the University, especially at the graduate level in psychology, biological sciences, and chemistry, are equally impressive. Medical School professors—perhaps somewhat surprisingly—have also had noticeable impact on undergraduate teaching. Ten or 12 are usually involved each year in the Freshman Seminars, a program of stimulating small-group classes. They were prominent in the initiation of the Human Biology Program, now one of the most popular

undergraduate majors, and as many as a dozen of them continue to teach in it.

The Stanford University Medical Center, designed by Edward Durell Stone, opened in 1959 on the campus with seven connecting pavilions built around pleasant courtyards. Since then an eighth pavilion for clinical sciences and an addition to the Stanford University Hospital have been joined to the original complex. The Louis B. Mayer Cancer Biology Research Laboratory and the Sherman Fairchild Center, housing the Neurobiology and Structural Biology Departments and an auditorium, have been erected nearby.

The School of Medicine portion of the center includes classrooms, laboratories, offices, and the 280,000-volume Lane Medical Library, the largest in the western United States. The 668-bed Stanford University Hospital (which includes Hoover Pavilion, formerly the Palo Alto Hospital) is both a regional hospital for referred patients with advanced medical problems and a community hospital for patients under the care of their own physicians. Inpatient days total about 167,000 a year. The Stanford University Clinics handle about 137,000 outpatient vis-

Oilcloth-covered tables and near-empty shelves furnished the first library of Cooper Medical College in San Francisco, predecessor of Stanford Medical School. The endowed Lane Medical Library (below) opened in 1906 with 10,000 volumes. Today it has 300,000 volumes and subscribes to 3,000 journals worldwide.

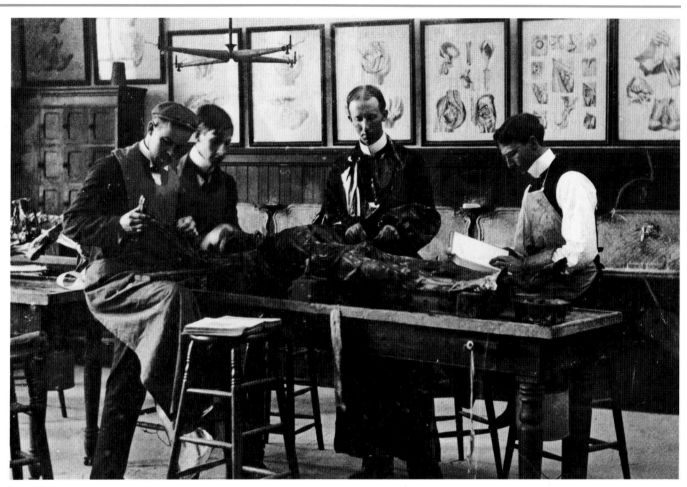

Ray Lyman Wilbur (second from left) in the anatomy laboratory of Cooper Medical College. Dr. Wilbur gave up a distinguished career in medicine to become president of Stanford.

its a year. The experience of both hospital and clinics has overcome early concerns that a suburban environment might not yield a sufficient number of patients for teaching needs.

Patient care is an extra dimension—in addition to teaching and research—that differentiates the Medical School from the rest of the University. It involves emotional, moral, and financial considerations—and it goes on seven days a week, year-round.

When the Medical Center was dedicated in 1959, the school could look back exactly 100 years to a lineal ancestor, the first medical school in California. Dr. Elias Samuel Cooper was the founder, and 13 students assembled for their first class in his San Francisco office in 1859. After Dr. Cooper's death his nephew, Dr. Levi Cooper Lane, reorganized the school in 1870, later naming it Cooper Medical College. Dr. Lane invested his own funds in a medical school building and a hospital in San Francisco.

With the turn of the century the era of virtuoso doctors in their frock coats administering to patients was rapidly giving way to a more scientific brand of medicine, and Dr. Lane shrewdly sensed that the future of medical education lay in affiliation with universities. In 1908, his college buildings having survived the 1906 earthquake, he transferred the assets of Cooper Medical College to Stan-

Built in the 1880s, this San Francisco brick building was the home of the Stanford Medical School before it moved to new quarters on the campus (overleaf).

137

ford without cost. Seven members of the Cooper faculty were appointed by Stanford to its new Department of Medicine. The eighth member was Dr. Ray Lyman Wilbur, who succeeded to the chairmanship of the department in 1911 and became dean when the department was made a school in 1913.

There were financial difficulties from the beginning and nonmedical faculty and the trustees were at odds over the ability of the University to bear the added operating costs. Dr. Branner, who had succeeded Dr. Jordan as president in 1913, proposed flatly to the trustees that the Medical School be abandoned and that "the entire equipment be turned over to the University of California upon such terms as the Trustees may be able to arrange." But an outside expert hired by the trustees advised them to keep the Medical School and this they resolved to do. By mid-1914 Dr. Wilbur was able to write, "We are quite relieved to have these various problems behind us, but have been sanguine throughout knowing that we would eventually land on our feet."

Dr. William Ophüls, a faculty member, succeeded Dr. Wilbur as dean in 1916 when Wilbur became president of the University. He retired in 1933 and his successor, Dr. Loren R. "Yank" Chandler, served until the decision of the Board of Trustees in 1953 to move the school to the Palo Alto campus. In the aging San Francisco facilities, these two men nurtured the school's reputation for clinical teaching and patient care. Strong departments of surgery, medicine, and pediatrics were built around professors the likes of Emile Holman, Arthur Bloomfield, George Barnett, and Harold Faber.

Just before the move Dr. Chandler wrote: "The School on Clay Street has lived a use-

ful and worthy life. Many superior physicians, considerable research of fundamental value, and two great groups of teachers have made Stanford Medical School's reputation outstanding during the past 40 years.... A new school, new in location, philosophy, objectives, curricula and with many new faces on the faculty, will be born in September 1959 on the Stanford campus. The King is dead. Long live the King!"

As Chandler predicted, the school grew and changed after the move. Full-time faculty members of professorial rank have increased from 116 to the current 288. The number of students pursuing the M.D. degree has nearly doubled to reach 380, and applicants for the 86 places in the entering class have reached nearly 6,000. The number of non-M.D. graduate students has increased almost five-fold to 158.

But the most far-reaching change has been the rise of basic research to a place of importance alongside clinical research, teaching, and patient care. "The primary commitment of both the school and hospital is to the im-

Stanford educated (A.B. '20, M.D. '23), Loren R. "Yank" Chandler joined the Medical School's faculty in 1923, and ten years after receiving his medical degree he was named the school's dean. He served in this post for 20 years, resigning when the Medical School planned its move from San Francisco to the campus in 1953.

From Washington University Medical School came Arthur Kornberg, cowinner of the 1959 Nobel Prize in Medicine for his work in synthesizing DNA, to head a new Department of Biochemistry at Stanford in 1959. Holder of the first Emma Pfeiffer Merner Professorship in the Medical Sciences, Kornberg is a member of the National Academy of Sciences and his work has opened the way to important progress in the study of genetics and virus infections and the nature of certain forms of cancer. Kornberg relinquished the department chairmanship in 1969 to return to research and teaching.

provement of medical education and patient care through the advance of medical knowledge," said Dr. Clayton Rich, who served as dean from 1971 through 1978. The creation of two new preclinical departments soon after the move points up the situation. The Biochemistry Department was formed with Arthur Kornberg, a Nobel Laureate, as its head. Its faculty gave Stanford the strongest group of molecular biologists in the world. Another Nobel Prize winner, Joshua Lederberg, came to Stanford to head the new Department of Genetics. (Lederberg has since become president of Rockefeller University.)

All but a few of the school's regular professors are involved in research investigations. The number of sponsored projects exceeds 500 and research awards approximate $35 million a year. To single out a few: Stanley N. Cohen's pioneering work in gene splicing, Hugh O. McDevitt's studies of heredity and the predisposition of individuals to disease, Henry S. Kaplan's work in the biology of cancer and development of treatments for Hodgkin's disease and other types of cancer,

Thomas C. Merigan's studies of the natural antiviral substance called interferon, Norman E. Shumway's heart transplantation research, Avram Goldstein's isolation of opiate receptors in the brain, and Arthur Kornberg's work on the laboratory manufacture of DNA, the complex molecule which controls heredity.

A high level of scientific investigation has been maintained at Stanford in the face of diminishing support nationally for basic research. Dr. Kornberg has stressed the need "to strengthen the scientific fiber and foundations of medicine." He argues: "The Medical School must, as a responsible technical school within the University, prepare its students with the basic knowledge, skills, and experience to be fully qualified practitioners of medicine. However, the central mission of the Medical School is to advance the knowledge of medicine and to imbue students with this spirit. By asking probing and penetrating questions that challenge a current dictum, we train the physician who will remain attentive to new knowledge and to whom you and I would entrust our families."

One of the major attractions of the Stanford School of Medicine is its flexible curriculum, which permits medical students to pursue specific research interests or obtain advanced degrees in other fields while studying for their medical degree. These first-year students are attending a preclinical anatomy laboratory.

THE FIRST HEART TRANSPLANT

The wedding guests had assembled when one of them, a member of the heart transplant team at the Stanford Medical Center, received an emergency call to report to the hospital. The long-planned first transplant in the United States of an adult human heart was about to take place.

It happened that another guest at the reception was a reporter for a local newspaper, and he quickly surmised what was happening. When his story broke, nearly 100 newspaper and TV people descended on the Medical Center in a matter of hours. The number soon swelled to 150 as reporters arrived from all over the world.

The Medical Center was prepared. Several months before the operation took place on January 6, 1968, the surgical team headed by Dr. Norman E. Shumway had completed eight years of animal research that demonstrated that transplantation of the heart was feasible. They decided to take the big step to human transplantation as soon as a patient and a donor heart could be matched. During the waiting period Dr. Shumway, Spyros Andreopoulos, Medical Center information officer, and other center officials established procedures for handling the story.

Meanwhile, surgeons in Capetown, South Africa—using techniques developed by the Shumway team—performed two cardiac transplants, and 'Newsweek' observed that "the medical significance of the event was being obscured by a circus atmosphere with Marx brothers overtones."

At Stanford the legion of reporters and television cameramen worked from a specially prepared pressroom, where bulletins were issued regularly and Dr. Shumway (white coat, arms folded) and other doctors appeared for interviews. The wife of the recipient granted an interview to a network wire service pool; otherwise the Information Office was the spokesman for relatives of donor and recipient. Andreopoulos and his staff put in two weeks of 12-hour days and sleepless nights before interest finally waned.

Unlike other medical centers, Stanford has maintained a regular program of cardiac transplantation, applying what has been learned on how to overcome the body's natural tendency to reject a foreign body. By the beginning of 1980 the Shumway team had performed 182 transplants and the rate of those surviving one year or longer had risen to 70 percent. One patient had survived 10 years. The procedure—once the object of such intense press attention—could become a routine life-extending treatment for some 75,000 Americans each year, a Stanford cardiologist has reported in the 'Journal of the American Medical Association.'

Centers of Research

Hopkins Marine Station

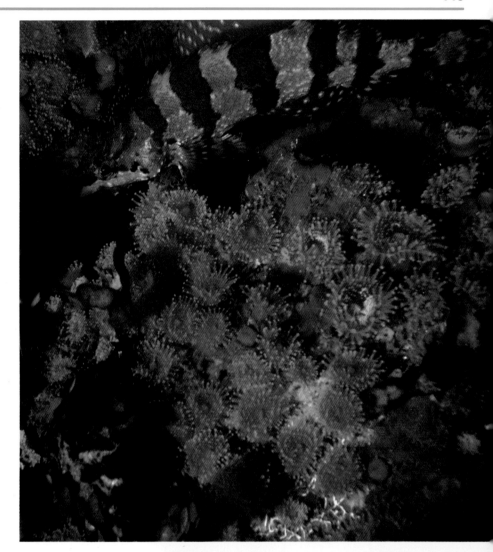

Hopkins Marine Station occupies 11 acres on Point Cabrillo in Pacific Grove, commanding a mile of shoreline along the scimitar curve of Monterey Bay. The granite reefs and outcroppings, sandy beaches, protected channels and tide pools, and offshore kelp forests support an immensely rich flora and fauna.

"Virtually every major group of animals has representatives within wading distance of the laboratory," says Colin S. Pittendrigh, station director. "The communities in this intact piece of nature can be, themselves, the object of natural historical or ecological research; they can provide the most appropriate organisms for studies of behavioral or physiological processes; or they can be a source of some uniquely suitable material for the most arcane laboratory analysis by biologists with little interest in their natural history."

The center of Monterey Bay is cleft by the mile-deep Monterey Submarine Canyon, the largest along the California coast, and oceanic fishes and invertebrates are easily obtained by trawling in its depths. Dredging on sand and shale bottoms in shallower water also provides a variety of organisms. Finally, within a radius of a few miles of the station are intertidal mudflats, brackish estuaries, brine pools, and protected harbor floats and pilings—the habitats of still other marine life.

"Visiting biologists at Monterey profess themselves astounded at the wealth of shore life," Walter K. Fisher, Hopkins director from 1918 to 1943, wrote in *Science*, adding that "the climate is never uncomfortably hot and irises bloom in the Station grounds at Christmas."

Stanford has been on Monterey Bay since 1892, the University's second year, thanks to the initiative of two young faculty members.

Above and right: Underwater scenes in Monterey Bay. Fish is called the convict fish, Oxylebius. *Small red plants with white tentacles are club-tipped anemone or gang anemone,* Corynactis. *Opposite: A class investigates the tidepools.*

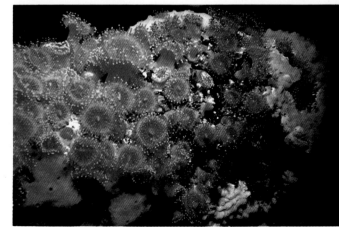

Oliver Peebles Jenkins, a physiologist, and Charles Henry Gilbert, a zoologist, took it upon themselves to scout the Pacific Coast for a suitable location. They settled on Point Aulon (now called Lover's Point), a treeless promontory that jutted into the sea at the "tidy little town" of Pacific Grove. The land, it turned out, was owned by the Pacific Improvement Company, a sort of holding company for the Southern Pacific Railroad. Timothy Hopkins, foster son of Mark Hopkins and a Stanford trustee, prevailed upon the company to give the point to Stanford and provided funds for the construction of a plain wooden laboratory building, 25 by 60 feet. Sixteen students came to the opening session the summer of 1892 and the Hopkins Seaside Laboratory, as it was originally called, became the first marine laboratory on the Pacific Coast of America and the third in the United States.

For the next 25 years the laboratory was open summers only and conditions were somewhat primitive. "We cooked our meals in the old laboratory, and slept there in sailcloths on the floor," remembered Harold Heath, an early faculty member. Ray Lyman Wilbur spent the summer of 1895 at Pacific

The summer class of 1894 poses in front of the wooden laboratory building on Lover's Point. The name was changed to Hopkins Marine Station at the time of the move to Cabrillo Point in 1917.

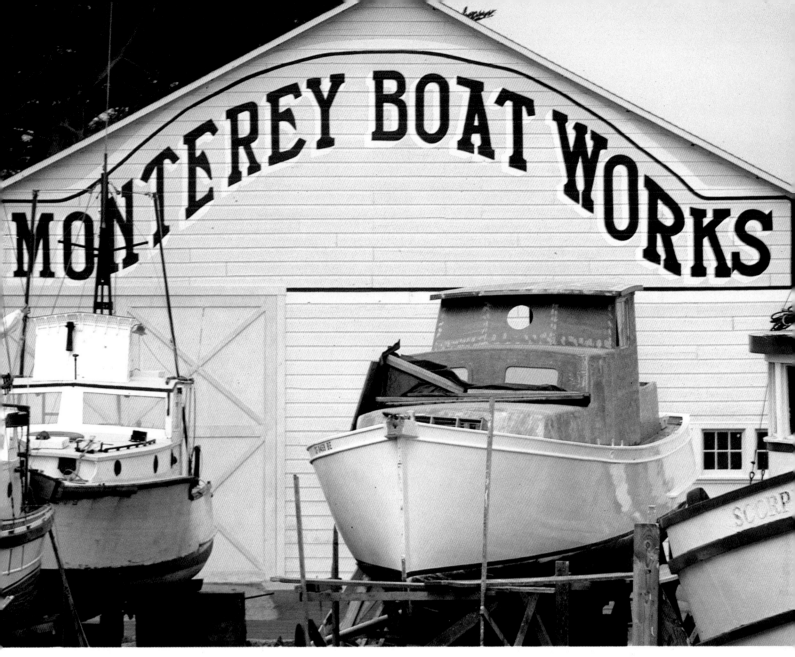

Above: The Monterey Boat Works, built in the early 1900s, originally housed a boat repair firm. It has been restored to house the station's diving headquarters, a new lecture hall, and the library. Left: Cannery Row, the haunt of John Steinbeck, edges the Marine Station. Cannery operations ceased in 1972.

A HUMBLE GENIUS

Cornelis B. van Niel, Hopkins Marine Station's near-legendary microbiologist, was shocked when he learned that President Lyndon Johnson had selected him, with four other distinguished American researchers, for the 1964 National Medal of Science. The brilliant, unassuming professor did not know he had been nominated for the honor by his colleagues in the National Academy of Sciences. "It came as a complete and utter surprise," he said. "I have worked in such isolation here."

Van Niel came to Hopkins in 1929 to continue studies begun at the Delft Institute in Holland. His discoveries clarified the basic mechanisms of photosynthesis.

As a teacher, van Niel was noted for his summer quarter course in microbiology, an intense 15-unit battery of lectures and laboratory work. He would sometimes lecture and demonstrate for eight hours at a stretch. Arthur Kornberg, later to become a Nobel Laureate for his work in DNA and member of the Stanford Medical School faculty, took the course in 1953 and credits it with arousing his interest in microbiology.

Van Niel, Norbert Weiner, John R. Pierce, Vannevar Bush, and L.W. Alvarez won the National Medal of Science in the award's second year, Theodor Von Karman having been the only previous winner. While cameras of the national network news programs ground, President Johnson read van Niel's citation, written in typical award jargon, then ad-libbed: "Anyone who can read a citation like that deserves a medal, too." The usually imperturbable van Niel smiled and bowed, ever so slightly.

Grove and recalled in his memoirs long days of collecting and supper parties on the beach. "I count this as one of the great experiences of my University career," he wrote.

By 1917 resort activities had encroached too close to Lover's Point and the laboratory was moved about a mile eastward to another Pacific Improvement Company property, the present site on Point Cabrillo. Again through the generosity of Timothy Hopkins, the laboratory later to be named for Alexander Agassiz was built. Professor Fisher became the first resident director of the renamed Hopkins Marine Station, and a year-round schedule was adopted.

Hopkins Marine Station, as part of the Department of Biological Sciences in the School of Humanities and Sciences, has made a strong contribution to research and teaching at Stanford. In the past 20 years some 20 percent of the Ph.D.'s in biology have done all or part of their thesis work at Hopkins. About 70 undergraduates study there during the year.

The famous "Spring Course" for undergraduates, widely copied in this country and abroad, was begun in 1963. It brings about 30 Stanford students to Pacific Grove where they rapidly find themselves putting in as many as 12 hours a day on individual research projects related to a general problem posed by the faculty. Some years the class has investigated the biology of a certain organism, other years it has taken on an ecological problem such as the impact of sewage disposal in the ocean on beach communities. The primary purpose is to teach researching. "Part of being a researcher," says Donald P. Abbott, one of the founders of the course, "is becoming so immersed in your problem that sometimes you can't sleep,

Isabella Abbott, professor of biological sciences at Hopkins, specializes in the study of red algae–their taxonomy, morphology, and reproduction. Coauthor of Marine Algae of California, *to date the most comprehensive guide to seaweeds of the Pacific Coast, Abbott received a dean's award for superior teaching from the School of Humanities and Sciences in 1978.*

and if you can, you dream about it." This happens easily in the comparative seclusion of the station.

In the mid-1970s, after an encouraging report by a visiting committee of distinguished scientists, the University administration decided to pump funds into enlarging the faculty and improving the aging station facilities. Professor Pittendrigh—internationally recognized for his studies of biological rhythms, known as "biological clocks," in animals—was appointed director in 1976. He has been a member of the Stanford biology faculty since 1969, coming from 22 years on the Princeton faculty. Two other outstanding appointments have been made, bringing the station complement to nine, and the director has also arranged for members of the University's Medical School to do research at Hopkins.

Pittendrigh has presided over the complete renovation of the Agassiz and Jacques Loeb laboratory buildings. A third laboratory building, built in 1963, has been renamed

the Lawrence Blinks Laboratory in honor of the man who joined the Hopkins faculty in 1931 and served as director from 1943 until he retired in 1965. The station's fourth major structure is the "Monterey Boat Works," a wooden landmark close by the Agassiz lab. Its picturesque exterior was preserved but inside it was completely rebuilt in 1977 to house the Walter K. Fisher Lecture Hall, the C.B. van Niel Library of Biological Sciences, and a suite of lockers and showers for scuba divers.

Hopkins is not large as marine stations go, but it has achieved remarkable stature for the quality of its teaching and research. It is remarkable, too, for another characteristic, defined by Pittendrigh: "For decades it has been the place where 'students' at all levels—undergraduate, graduate, postdoctoral, and faculty—have found that they could do their work, close to marine life, in an atmosphere of great tradition, physical beauty, and tranquility. It has been a place that generates loyalty and gratitude."

The Agassiz Laboratory, with the landing beach for small research craft in the foreground.

Hoover Institution on War, Revolution and Peace

The Herbert Hoover Federal Memorial, the only memorial to a former president of the United States placed by Congress on the Pacific Coast and the only one on a major university campus, is not a monument chiseled in stone. It is a living memorial that provides educational facilities wherein scholars can carry forward Hoover's unrelenting search for a stable, peaceful world.

Dedicated in 1978, the memorial integrates additional buildings with the landmark tower and other facilities of the Hoover Institution on War, Revolution and Peace. Together they house a library and archive on social, political, and economic change in the twentieth century that is unrivaled in size and richness by any other private collection in the nation. They also provide working space for resident researchers, visiting scholars from all over the world, visiting fellows, and an active publications program.

"If we were inclined to boast, which, of course, we are not, I would say the new building complex will provide us with physical facilities unequaled by any other similar center in this country," W. Glenn Campbell, Hoover Institution director, declared at the groundbreaking.

Hoover, who maintained an office on the eleventh floor of the tower until his death in 1964, first thought of founding the library at his alma mater while crossing the North Sea during World War I. As director of the Commission for Relief in Belgium, he made 40 crossings of the choppy, mine-sown waters in small, obsolete Dutch steamers. He wrote in his memoirs: "On one of these North Sea crossings I read in one of Andrew D. White's writings that most of the fugitive literature of comment during the French Revolution was lost to history because no one set any value on

it at the time, and that without such material it became very difficult or impossible to reconstruct the real scene. Therein lay the origins of the Library... at Stanford University."

While the war still raged Hoover lined up professional collectors in the capitals of all belligerents to gather such fugitive material as propaganda leaflets, newspapers, government documents, and periodicals, and hold them until peace came. Immediately after the Armistice Professor E.D. Adams of the Stanford History Department went to Europe, where Hoover personally provided him with a credit of $50,000 to pursue the collecting. He was aided by a dozen or more young men with experience as history teachers who were released from the army to the project by General Pershing. "They were overjoyed to get out of billets and went at it with a vim," Hoover related. As carloads of material arrived in ports, Hoover, by then director of the American Relief Administration, saw to it that they were loaded onto returning ships which had brought food from America.

The collecting pace did not slacken. When Hoover, through the ARA, undertook to feed

The Hoover Tower (opposite) rises 285 feet into the campus skyline. Dedicated in 1941 during the University's 50th anniversary celebration, it is the central structure of the Hoover Institution's complex. Herbert Hoover, founder of the Institution (shown here in a 1951 photograph), used to occupy his eleventh-floor tower office regularly during the month of July.

An enlarged casting of Hoover's official presidential medal centers the exhibition pavilion of the Herbert Hoover Federal Memorial adjacent to the tower.

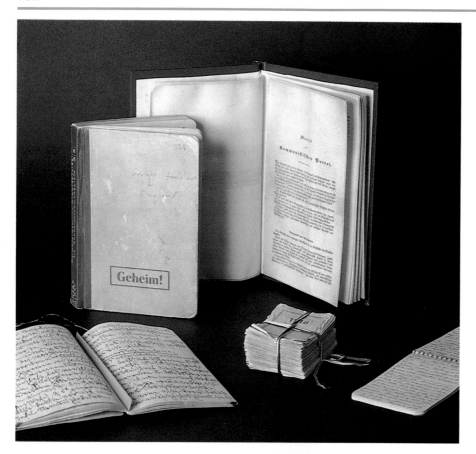

millions of famine-stricken Russians in 1921, a Hoover Institution representative, though frequently tailed by Communist secret police, gathered records of the last days of the tsarist regime, the short-lived provisional government, and early revolutionary years. Others, meanwhile, were crossing and recrossing Western and Central Europe, gathering material on the Paris Peace Conference, economic reconstruction, and the rise of left- and right-wing organizations, including extensive information on the Nazi party.

Hoover Institution representatives, provided with funds ahead of time, were again on the job during World War II. In 1946 President Truman appointed Hoover to coordinate world efforts to alleviate the great famines which inevitably follow war. He visited 39 countries and returned with hundreds of now valuable documents. General MacArthur delegated several members of his staff to devote full time to collecting Japanese materials for Hoover. Chiang Kai-shek's government gave him materials on the Nationalists' war effort, and in Berlin he was presented with a diary of Nazi propaganda chief Joseph Goebbels. Many Stanford alumni, faculty members, and students who had been in the armed services also contributed material. An alumnus who was a leader of Filipino guerrilla forces sent Hoover Institution a large collection on the occupation, including a complete set of the journals from the Japanese military government in the Philippines.

Since World War II, and particularly with a new infusion of funds that followed the appointment of Campbell as director in 1959, the collections have grown steadily in size and geographical range. The original concentrations on Eastern and Western Europe

Treasures from the Hoover Institution archives (clockwise from lower left): Heinrich Himmler's diary; Gestapo arrest list in anticipation of invasion of England; rare first edition, probably the only one in the U.S., of the Communist Manifesto; prison diary of a German revolutionary written in code on a calendar pad; one of 50 pocket diaries of General Joseph W. Stillwell in the Hoover collections.

Seymour Martin Lipset, professor of political science and sociology, is a senior fellow at Hoover Institution. A leading pollster on social issues, Lipset won the Gunnar Myrdal Award in 1971 for his book The Politics of Unreason: Right-Wing Extremism in America 1790-1970. *He is a member of the National Academy of Sciences and former vice-president of the American Academy of Arts and Sciences.*

have been maintained and the holdings on Africa and the Middle East, East Asia, and Latin America have been greatly strengthened. "Hoover's pack rats," as the overseas collectors have always been called, are constantly on the lookout for appropriate materials, and curators make regular collecting pilgrimages.

The institution's library holdings approximate 1.5 million books, pamphlets, and government documents from more than 100 countries. The archives contain some 4,000 individual collections of unpublished primary source material, ranging from a single sheet of paper to a collection weighing 20 tons and stored in 1,800 boxes.

From the beginning the library and archives have been open to everyone with a serious

A Russian naval officer's sword and other examples from the archive's large collection of Czarist Russian memorabilia. Left: Peace buttons, primarily World War I era, from the Alice Park Collection.

Top: Three of the 520 military decorations in the Jack Goldman Collection. The middle one is known as the Blue Max. Above: An arcade of the Lou Henry Hoover Building.

interest: students, scholars, and writers. No restrictions have been placed on the use of materials. Hoover once said that the institution's collections are "as free as the Sierra winds for historians to interpret as they see fit." For the past several years well over 1,000 visiting scholars have come annually from around the world for days, weeks, or months of study. Alexander Kerensky, the premier of Russia's 1917 provisional government, spent several years at the institution preparing a three-volume history of his regime. A more recent visitor was Alexander Solzhenitsyn. Among popular writers have been Barbara Tuchman (*The Guns of August* and *Stillwell and the American Experience in China: 1911-1945*) and William L. Shirer (*The Rise and Fall of the Third Reich*).

The institution's resident staff consists of some 140 scholars, curators, archivists, librarians, and research assistants, who speak a total of 41 languages. It includes specialists in economics, education, history, political science, philosophy, sociology, and international law. Three Nobel Laureates are associated with the Hoover Institution—senior research fellow Milton Friedman and two honorary fellows, Solzhenitsyn and international economist Friedrich A. Hayek.

During the institution's first 50 years, collecting and research focused primarily on international affairs. In 1971 its board of overseers endorsed a plan to expand into domestic studies of such problems as immigration, health care, social security, welfare reform, federal regulation of industry, and drug abuse. The resident research staff members are now divided almost equally between international and domestic studies, with a strong orientation toward analysis of the public policy issues facing society. The Hoover Institution Press, which issues about 25 new titles a year, disseminates their research results, as do outside publishers, and they also make their views known through speeches, by-lined articles, and appearances at congressional hearings.

The National, Peace, and Public Affairs Fellows Program frees about a dozen young scholars from around the country to spend a year in advanced research at the institution. They also participate in seminars and informal discussions and generally rub elbows with their senior colleagues.

When Congress appropriated funds for the Herbert Hoover Federal Memorial in 1975, it stated that the memorial was to take the form of educational facilities at the Hoover Institution. The appropriateness of this action was underscored by President Lyman at the groundbreaking ceremony: "It's very auspicious, I think, that this memorial to the late President Hoover should be located in the heart of a major private university, the one that he himself attended . . . ; for this memorial will be more than a fine and useful building; it will be a center for the active life of the mind, the fostering of which is the primary purpose of a university."

Solzhenitsyn, seated in Herbert Hoover's former office, makes notes in the tiny, paper-saving script that he learned to use while in Russian prison camps.

SOLZHENITSYN AT THE HOOVER

On the same day in 1974 that Alexander Solzhenitsyn was abruptly exiled from his homeland by Soviet authorities, Stanford president Richard W. Lyman and Hoover Institution director W. Glenn Campbell cabled him: "Please know that should you desire to continue your research and writing, we will do all that we can to facilitate your work and to accommodate you and your family."

The answer was a little more than a year in coming. Late in May 1975, Solzhenitsyn called from Alaska that he would be at the Hoover Institution in three days. The Nobel Laureate and his wife, Natalia, closeted themselves in the same redwood-paneled office on the eleventh floor of the Hoover Tower that had been Herbert Hoover's. They worked 12 hours a day without breaking for lunch, while two archivists brought the material the author needed for his history of Russia in 1917.

Solzhenitsyn was not unfamiliar with the institution's resources. "For years the Hoover Institution had been supplying him with copies of documents from our archive materials on Russia," explains Richard Staar, associate director of the institution and Solzhenitsyn's host and interpreter.

At the end of his stay Solzhenitsyn accepted appointment as an honorary fellow of the Hoover Institution. He said, "The documentation I have examined is outstanding and, in many respects, unique. Materials dated prior to 1922 are especially well represented here. It is the kind of original source material that the Soviets, in order to rewrite history, either destroyed or refuse to make available to scholars. I look forward to utilizing your special collections and library materials for the rest of my life."

Food Research Institute

"We study the tides, not the waves." That's the way Walter P. Falcon, director of the Food Research Institute, describes the institute's careful and sustained approach to investigations of the production, distribution, and consumption of food on a global scale.

"Our work is not aimed at the faddish topics of the moment. Rather we try for a long-run, thorough understanding, with a strong commitment to facts and to the empirical method. We have a staid tradition."

As a consequence the Food Research Institute has built up and made widely available a comprehensive body of knowledge about world food supplies and requirements since it was established right after World War I. In fact, it was the woeful lack of such information to aid his work in feeding Europe during and after the war that led Herbert Hoover to secure initial financing for the institute from the Carnegie Corporation of New York.

When he went to see James R. Angell, president of the Carnegie Corporation, Hoover took with him Alonzo E. Taylor, a nutrition expert who had been one of his top staff men during the wartime relief work in Europe. Angell asked Hoover to send him a list of projects that such an institution might undertake for submission to his board, and Hoover began his reply, "I can enumerate at least fifty important matters that are really vital to the economic and health development of the United States." He listed quite a few, then wrote, "I could go on for some time."

The Carnegie board apparently was impressed, for it granted the project $50,000 for each of the first two years, $70,000 for each of the next eight years, and then, satis-

fied that the value of the Food Research Institute had been demonstrated, handed the Stanford trustees an endowment fund of $750,000.

The institute opened in July of 1921. Three coequal directors were appointed: Dr. Taylor, the nutritionist; Carl L. Alsberg, a biochemist who was head of the Federal Bureau of Chemistry; and Joseph S. Davis, a Harvard economist.

Prudent ways have not kept the institute from pioneering research into areas of applied economics which later have become matters of great national concern. Reports former director William O. Jones, "The institute staff has been free to investigate problems that have not yet seized the public interest and to report their findings, however con-

The west wing of Encina Hall was completely remodeled, including a new arched entryway, for the Food Research Institute in 1970. It was in the basement of this wing, when Encina was the freshman men's dormitory, that the legendary "Blackie" held forth in the Encina Cellar snack bar.

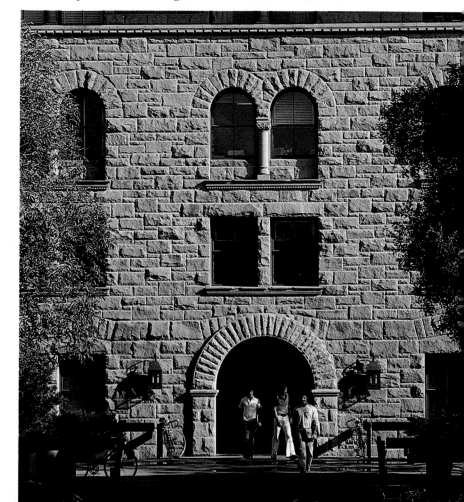

trary they might be to received doctrine." Studies of Soviet agriculture and the world wheat economy were begun in the 1930s; analysis of the United States population upsurge was started in the 1940s; and investigations of the economic behavior of small-scale farmers were initiated in the 1950s. During World War II institute faculty members served the American government directly by analyzing the wartime food situation in occupied Europe and by administering food and agricultural programs of the United States and its allies.

Since the 1960s the institute has directed an increasing proportion of its resources to world food problems, especially those of Africa and other Third World regions. One new project emphasizes the integration of nutrition, health, and family-planning programs as a strategy for rural development. Others deal with the world rice economy, agricultural change in tropical Africa, the efficiency of Asian agriculture, the operation of futures markets for agricultural products, and rural development within Mexico.

Although staff members have always taught classes in addition to their research work, the Food Research Institute did not become a formal academic unit of the University until 1933. It is now a department of the School of Humanities and Sciences. Typically there are 40 students in residence, more than one-third from outside the United States, mostly from developing countries. Usually six to eight Ph.D.'s and about a dozen A.M.'s are awarded each year. A joint master's degree in international agricultural economics is offered with the Graduate School of Business. Although an undergraduate major is not available, all of the institute's 14 scholars teach undergraduate courses, which are cross-listed with other departments of the University.

Members of the faculty are also active as consultants and advisers to numerous national and international groups, public and private, such as the United Nations, Chicago Board of Trade, Ford Foundation, Agency for International Development, and regulatory commissions. They frequently work overseas in collaboration with researchers on the faculties of Third World universities. Recently the institute's director was appointed by President Carter as one of 14 members of a Presidential Commission on World Hunger, which seeks to improve understanding of the problem and to devise ways for the United States to help combat it. Falcon has also traveled to the People's Republic of China and is a coauthor of two assessments of the efforts of the Chinese to solve their food shortages.

When the Institute moved in 1970 from its longtime quarters on the Inner Quad to the newly remodeled west wing of Encina Hall, Joseph S. Davis, the only survivor of the original directors, called on his memories: "Despite differences in age, background, and experience the directors happily complemented one another and worked harmoniously together.... We very early agreed to focus on the economics of food and agriculture, with ample recognition of non-economic disciplines such as chemistry, nutrition, geography, history, demography, and statistics....

"Mr. Hoover, an assiduous promoter of research, liked to say: 'Get the facts.' Our previous experience had made us realize that this is no simple task.... Unsparingly honest and painstaking interpretation is vital. The great need, we felt, was for facts, organized into knowledge, maturing into wisdom."

Internationally known demographer Dudley Kirk held the first Dean and Virginia Morrison Professorship in Population Studies until his retirement in 1979. Kirk came to Stanford in 1967 as professor of demography as well as to teach in the Department of Sociology. He was the first official appointed for policy and research on world population problems at the State Department, where he served for seven years, and continues to do research on population problems that are of crucial world concern.

Stanford Linear Accelerator Center

Deep within the rolling ground of the Stanford Linear Accelerator Center, revolutionary research in elementary particle physics is taking place. First, a beam of electrons and a following beam of their antiparticles, the positrons, are accelerated to nearly the speed of light down a slender two-mile-long copper tube. The two beams are then circulated in counter-rotating directions in a vacuum storage ring more than a mile in circumference. When giant magnets cause the racing beams to meet head-on, some of the opposing particles collide with and annihilate each other in infinitesimally small fireballs of pure electromagnetic energy that is hotter and more densely concentrated than almost anything else known in the universe. This concentrated energy instantly rematerializes into showers of subnuclear particles whose properties are measured and recorded by huge electronic detectors.

The storage ring, called PEP (Positron Electron Project), is new. Parts of it were first tested late in 1979. The two-mile accelerator (SLAC), in terms of the fast-moving world of high-energy physics, is old. It has been operating with great success since 1966. Hooked in tandem, PEP and the accelerator are expected to advance the new age of quantum dynamics, perhaps providing a key step forward in the search begun by Einstein for a single set of equations to explain all of nature's basic forces.

PEP is a big brother of SPEAR (Stanford Positron Electron Asymmetric Ring), a colliding beam facility ten times smaller, which began operation in 1972. SPEAR really started the revolution. A team of physicists from SLAC and the University of California's Lawrence Berkeley Laboratory used the SPEAR ring to discover in November 1974

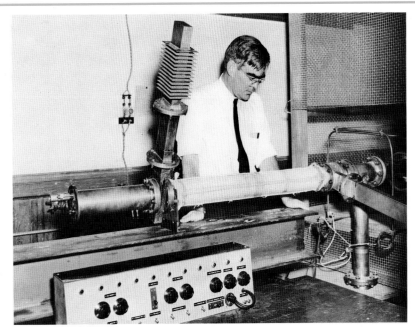

a wholly new and unsuspected family of subnuclear particles, the psions, which opened a view of the structure of matter more fundamental than any seen before. The finding set off an epidemic of excitement among those working in the field. "Hardly ever, if ever," reported the *New York Times*, "has physics been in such an uproar as during the last three weeks, and the end is not in sight."

SLAC's Professor Burton Richter, head of the SPEAR experimental group, spent more than ten years on the design, funding, and construction of SPEAR. For his part in the discovery of the first psi particle, he shared the 1976 Nobel Prize for physics. The discovery "has changed the work-style of laboratories throughout the world," according to a spokesman for the Swedish Royal Academy, which awards the Nobel Prize. "A new field of research has been opened."

If SPEAR is so good, why PEP?

PEP exists because, as with most major scientific discoveries, SPEAR's findings raised almost as many questions as they answered.

Opposite: From the target area and research yard in the foreground, the SLAC tunnel stretches two miles to the distant point where electrons are shot into its slender copper tube. Midway, Highway 280 makes a crossing. The underground PEP ring, more than a mile around, completely encircles the research yard. Above: William W. Hansen in a Stanford physics laboratory with the first three-foot-long electron linear accelerator, developed in 1947.

SAM AND J AND BURT AND PSI

Burton Richter of SLAC and Samuel C.C. Ting of M.I.T. were jointly awarded the Nobel Prize in 1976 for their simultaneous discovery of an entirely new elementary particle.

The fact that their two teams, using different methods and working on opposite coasts, made identical discoveries of a revolutionary nature is a strange enough story. But the way they found this out is even stranger.

Ting arrived at SLAC for a committee meeting the morning after the SLAC/Lawrence Berkeley Laboratory group had verified its finding. Richter picks up the story:

"When I met Sam early that morning, he said to me, 'Burt, I have some interesting physics to tell you about.' My response was, 'Sam, I have some interesting physics to tell you about!'

"What this conversation lacked in sparkle it more than made up for in astonishing coincidence, for it soon became clear that Ting's group had discovered the very same particle in their experiment at Brookhaven."

The M.I.T./Brookhaven group called the particle "J" and the SLAC/LBL group named it "psi." After some friendly competition, in which emblazoned T-shirts played a part, the particle is now usually referred to as "J-psi."

The basic puzzles remain: What is the nature of matter at its simplest level? What are the fundamental particles of matter, and how do they interact? The answers require higher interaction energies, and PEP will provide more than four times the energy of SPEAR.

"In high-energy physics you have to have bigger and bigger machines to see smaller and smaller things," SLAC's director, W.K.H. Panofsky, remarked some 20 years ago when the two-mile accelerator was under construction, and the statement still holds true.

Although the ideas developed by a good many scientists over a good many years were involved, it is correct to say that the electron linear accelerator was invented at Stanford shortly after World War II and that William W. Hansen, a member of the Stanford physics faculty, was the man chiefly responsible. Hansen, who had worked on the early development of the klystron tube, and his associates were searching for a simpler and more powerful type of accelerator for bombarding the atom in order to deduce its structure. In 1947 they operated their first model, a three-foot-long tube that generated a 1.5-million-electron-volt beam. Hansen put his whole report to his sponsor, the U.S. Office of Research and Inventions, into four words: "We have accelerated electrons."

Meanwhile, Stanford professors Marvin Chodorow and Edward L. Ginzton had succeeded in boosting dramatically the power of the klystron, the microwave tube invented at Stanford by the Varian brothers. In 1950 a billion-electron-volt accelerator, using klystrons as the source of the high-frequency radio waves which push the electrons down the tube, was put in operation. (Hansen, just entering his forties, had died the year before

The concrete tunnel is buried under 25 feet of compacted soil. The shed at ground level contains 240 klystron tubes for accelerating the subterranean beam.

and Ginzton became the project leader.) Using the new machine, called the Mark III, Professor Robert Hofstadter of the Stanford Department of Physics won the Nobel Prize in 1961 for his studies of electron scattering in atomic nuclei and for his discoveries concerning the structure of nucleons.

It was Hofstadter who first suggested that an accelerator 10 to 20 times more powerful than the Mark III be considered. The awesomeness of the proposed machine, which would be two miles in length, can be detected in its first nickname, "The Monster," later changed to "Project M." The first formal Project M meeting was held on April 10, 1956, in the home of Professor Panofsky, who had joined the Stanford faculty in 1952 and was to become director of SLAC in 1959. The minutes of this meeting record an interesting sentence: "The participation of the members of this group is entirely voluntary and on their own time as there are no funds available to support this program."

A detailed proposal for construction of Project M on Stanford land was presented to the federal government by President Sterling in 1957. After prolonged investigations and hearings—punctuated by President Eisenhower's endorsement in a nationally broadcast radio address—Congress authorized the Stanford Linear Accelerator Center project in 1961. A contract was signed between the Atomic Energy Commission and Stanford calling for the University to design the accelerator, build it on a 480-acre strip of land in the low foothills behind the campus, paralleling Sand Hill Road, and operate it. The huge job was completed in 1966, on schedule and within the allocated budget of $114 million.

Within a few months after the first beam of electrons was transmitted over the accelerator's full two-mile length, the projected energy of 20 billion electron volts was achieved. This has since been boosted to 24 billion. The electrons, injected at the beginning of the accelerator pipe, are driven constantly forward by microwaves fed into the pipe by regularly spaced klystron tubes. Answering to laws of physics, the electrons quickly approach the barrier speed of light (within 0.0000001 percent) and then increase in mass some 40,000 times. These superelectrons crash into the nuclei of stationary target material in two large end-station buildings, and the telltale scattering of the subnuclear particles created is studied in optical and electronic detectors. A SLAC experiment of this kind provided the first clear evidence that protons and neutrons in the nucleus of the atom are not the smallest particles of matter but rather are formed from particles which have come to be called quarks.

The coupling on of the SPEAR and PEP colliding beam rings has added a new dimension of power to the linear accelerator.

Sculpture-like components of the linear accelerator were displayed at the Stanford Museum in 1966. Above, a waveguide valve, part of the mechanism for transmitting klystron power to the speeding electrons. Below, cylinders and disks like these, more than 80,000 of each, are brazed together alternately to form the two-mile-long, four-inch-diameter accelerator tube.

Overleaf: Inside End Station A. This experimental hall is seven stories high and has a floor area of 25,000 square feet. Its huge spectrometers detect the scattering of electrons after they have bombarded target materials.

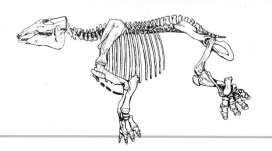

A skeleton unearthed during the SLAC construction proved to be that of a heavily built amphibian 15 million years old, now called Paleoparadoxia. Only one other had been found before—in Japan in 1961.

Energy, as highway accidents demonstrate, is doubled in head-on collisions. Thus PEP is able to deliver 36 billion electron volts initially and a considerable increase is expected after trials.

Yet each technique—the bombardment of fixed targets and the collision of beams—has its special uses and SLAC research will continue to use both of them.

The storage ring story began in 1958 when a Stanford-Princeton team constructed a machine in Stanford's High Energy Physics Laboratory that brought two electron beams into collision. Burton Richter, a recent M.I.T. Ph.D., was a junior member of the team. He became convinced that an electron-positron collision would be more productive than the electron-electron mode. (He said at the time of receiving the Nobel Prize: "I have been led on by a naive picture: positron and electron, particle and antiparticle, annihilating and forming a state of simple quantum numbers and enormous energy density from which all of the elementary particles could be formed.")

Richter and a colleague, Professor David Ritson, designed SPEAR for SLAC but could not get a federal agency to back it. The funds were finally squeezed out of SLAC's budget. The Stanford group, joined by Lawrence Berkeley Laboratory physicists who concentrated on devising the detection equipment, placed SPEAR in operation in 1973. A year later they discovered the psi particle. Richter has described SPEAR's $5.3 million price tag as "the biggest bargain in physics."

It became an even bigger bargain when the Stanford Synchrotron Radiation Laboratory was formed to take advantage of a SPEAR by-product—the extremely pure and intense X-

In the underground tunnel, the smaller accelerator tube is supported by the large, lower pipe. A laser beam is shot through optical targets in the lower pipe to align the accelerating structure to a tolerance of four-hundredths of an inch over its entire length.

ray and ultraviolet radiation thrown off by the electron beam as it is bent by magnets into its circular orbit. This radiation is siphoned off through slits in the ring and is used as an ideal illuminating source for looking at the structural details of all kinds of materials, including biological samples such as nerve, retinal, and muscle tissues. Some 300 scientists from around the country soon were using the facility. Although closely allied with SLAC, SSRL is an independent unit within the University and is supported by the National Science Foundation. Arthur I. Bienenstock, professor of materials science engineering, is director.

Today SLAC has 1,200 employees—one-third scientists and engineers, one-third technical and support personnel, and one-third administrative, clerical, and other workers. Its sponsoring agency is the Department of Energy. As a national facility engaged in no classified research, SLAC is open to researchers from all over the world, and usually at least half of the users are from outside Stanford. Panofsky expects this outside usage to increase because SLAC, the Brookhaven National Laboratory on Long Island, and Fermi National Accelerator Laboratory in Illinois have survived to become the three major centers for elementary particle physics experimentation in the United States.

So it has turned out that SLAC, in operation since 1966 and once thought by some to be too much "The Monster" to be able to adapt to emerging conditions, has kept very much in the front line of elementary particle physics. In his "state of SLAC" message for fiscal year 1980, Director Panofsky said, "There is no other electron accelerator in the world that even approaches SLAC's performance."

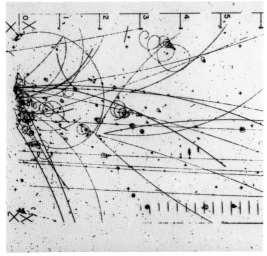

A 600-ton magnet, part of the PEP colliding beam apparatus, being moved into position at SLAC. Left: At the target end of the accelerator tube, subatomic particles leave visible tracks in the form of bubbles when they are fed into a chamber of liquid hydrogen.

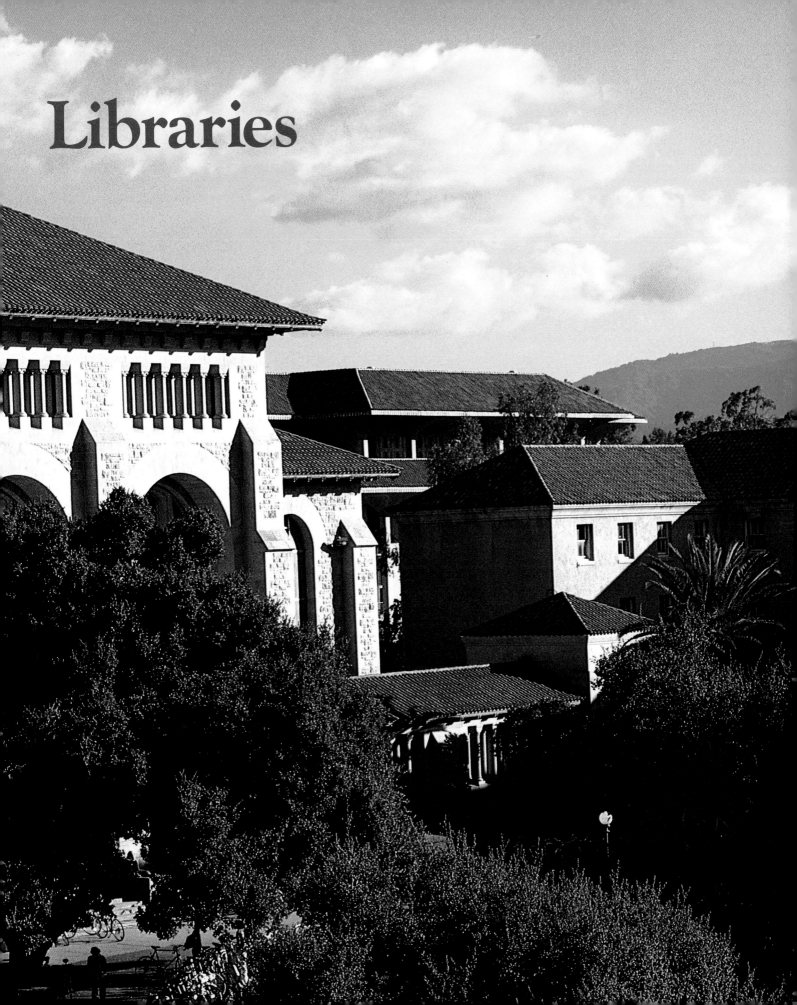

Libraries

university campus is not the best place to look for unanimity, but everyone seems to agree on one thing: there must be a great library.

President Lyman described the library as "the center of things, the treasury of human wisdom and knowledge, the source of countless adventures of the mind and spirit."

Without a fine library, a university is "a bloodless, a lifeless thing," observed Lawrence V. Ryan, professor of English and humanities.

"The magic of a library is that it integrates the work of the past as a base for the future," David C. Weber, director of the Stanford University Libraries, said.

And a good many years ago J. Pearce Mitchell, longtime registrar, boiled it down to "faculties and students need books, and then more books."

"More books" indeed. Stanford started life with a library of 3,000 volumes, crammed, with a few tables and chairs, into one small building on the Inner Quad. On rainy mornings there was standing room only, the first librarian, Edwin Hamlin Woodruff, lamented.

In 1975 the University Libraries celebrated the acquisition of their four millionth book, but conditions had not altered. Books were still overflowing the shelves, and space for sitting was at a premium.

As the seventies turned into the eighties, all of that changed with the dedication of a clean, efficient, and handsome addition to the Main Library that roughly doubled the

The first Stanford library was squeezed into one small building on the Inner Quad (below).

The immense reading room of the Main Library was a place for studying at a scholarly pace. Not so in the old Reserve Book Room on the first floor. There much-needed books were loaned for one or two hours, inexorably measured out by the big clock on the wall.

floor space and book capacity and tripled the seating and study provisions of the central facility. The enlarged building has been renamed the Cecil H. Green Library. Dr. and Mrs. Green were the principal donors toward the cost of the addition—"a noble gift," President Lyman said at the groundbreaking.

During that first hectic summer of 1891 when President Jordan, in the space of a few short weeks, was breathing life into the University, Leland Stanford cabled him, "To start in with I think a library such as a gentleman would have for his own use . . . would be sufficient." Jordan hastily built the library's first collection of 3,000 volumes largely from the gifts of faculty appointees. Another 3,000 were added by purchase during the first year and 2,000 more by a gift from Timothy Hopkins. During the third year, using the proceeds from a great fair in which the whole University took part, the library purchased a collection on German philology of 4,600 volumes and more than 1,000 pamphlets.

Following the death of Senator Stanford in 1893, his brother Thomas Welton Stan-

ford returned to the University his inheritance from the Senator's estate and this money was used to build a new library, the first building on the Outer Quadrangle. On January 19, 1900, classes were dismissed and students moved 50,000 volumes to the new Thomas Welton Stanford Library, where marble staircases led to a mezzanine guarded by intricately wrought metal railings, and three huge stained-glass windows on religious themes overlooked the loan desk.

Mrs. Stanford, wishing to complete in her lifetime all of the major structures she thought the University would need, soon authorized the construction of a separate library building on the site today occupied by the Graduate School of Business. The unhappy story of the planning of her library building and its destruction in the 1906 earthquake on the eve of its completion is told in an earlier chapter. But Mrs. Stanford's generosity toward the University's library continued after her death. She left her collection of jewels to the trustees with instructions that they were to be sold to endow the Jewel Fund for the purchase of books. The income from this half-million-dollar fund is still a major book-buying resource.

"By 1913 the congestion in the Thomas Welton Stanford Library had become embarrassing," according to Orrin Leslie Elliott. Somewhat delayed by World War I, the Main Library was opened in 1919. At the dedication John Maxon Stillman, one of the Old Guard faculty members, predicted that the new library "would give adequate accommodation for fifty years to come." He was almost right. By 1966 the Main Library, after much crowding out of staff and student study space, had reached the absolute limit of its book capacity. Only the existence of unused stacks

Thomas Welton Stanford (left), the Senator's brother, donated funds for a library that opened on the Outer Quad in 1900 (above). This space is now occupied by the Political Science Department. Right: Card catalogs took over the Main Library rotunda.

in the basement of the J. Henry Meyer Memorial Library for undergraduates, completed in 1966 adjacent to the Main Library, bought the University enough breathing time to remedy the situation.

The new and old sections of the Green Library are completely integrated at all four levels and are connected at the basement level to the Meyer library stacks. Together they provide 68 miles of shelving, enough for more than 2.8 million volumes, and seating for 1,700 readers. The biggest change effected by the addition has been to put the reader in the midst of the collection—that is, to replace the old closed stacks with open stacks.

Once qualified users have passed through the portal, the whole resources of the library are open to them. "This new concept stimulates serendipity as readers browse among the collections," Philip C. Williams, the University's director of planning, points out.

Small reading areas—tables and chairs, lounge-type facilities, or carrels—are scattered throughout the stacks. The lounge-type areas, which have been developed in five color schemes, are about the size of a large living room in a home.

The stepped bays of the addition partially enclose a library courtyard that is also bordered by the Meyer undergraduate library and

Above, left: The J. Henry Meyer Memorial Library for undergraduates. Above: This sculpture of Napoleon on Elba, brooding over a map of Europe, is in the Central Map Collection room. Right: Vaults and pillars in the old section of Green Library.

Above: This addition has been coupled to the old Main Library and the whole is now named the Cecil H. Green Library. Left: The tapestry, Wordscape, by Helena Hernmarck, hangs the full length of the library's three-story, open stairwell. Its vistas and fragments of the titles of great works express the limitless quality of the printed word.

the Education Building. This landscaped area provides a quiet "eddy space" for study and relaxation.

The Green Library is the flagship of the University Libraries system. Its new section houses the central card catalog, the reference rooms, humanities and social sciences research collections, and administrative offices. More commodiously resettled in the stately rooms of the old section are Special Collections, including rare books and manuscripts, the Stanford University Archives, Government Documents, the Map Collections, and Technical Services.

The books and periodicals most used by undergraduates are in the nearby J. Henry Meyer Memorial Library, and there are 11 research branches located in schools and departments: Art and Architecture, Cubberley Education, Music, Branner Earth Sciences, Computer Sciences, Engineering, Falconer Biology, Hopkins Marine Station, Mathematical Sciences, Physics, and Swain Library of Chemistry and Chemical Engineering.

There are also six coordinate libraries, administered independently: the library of the Food Research Institute, the library of the Hoover Institution, J. Hugh Jackson Library of Business, Lane Medical Library, School of Law Library, and the library of the Stanford Linear Accelerator Center.

In all of its libraries, Stanford has 4.5 million volumes, ranking seventh among academic institutions in the United States. Stanford also subscribes to 50,000 periodicals and holds 144,000 maps, 27.5 million manuscripts, and 1.6 million microtexts. The libraries acquire more than 7,000 books a month, on the average. The collections are doubling every 16 years and might, therefore, exceed 8 million volumes by 1995.

Above: The reference services desk of Green Library. Left: A literary tea in the Bender Room.

Since 1972 the processes of acquisition, receiving, and cataloguing have in large measure been automated so that books can be put to use promptly. This is done by a computerized system, the Research Libraries Information Network, for technical processing and collection access. RLIN was originated and developed by the Stanford University Libraries and has now been adopted by more than 120 research, academic, public, and special libraries, including UC-Berkeley, Yale, Columbia, and the New York Public Library.

RLIN also facilitates part of a cooperative program of unprecedented scope begun in 1976 by the libraries of Stanford and UC-

A VICTORIAN-AGE FEMINIST

Carl N. Degler, Margaret Byrne Professor of American History, was working in the Stanford University Archives when he experienced the dream of every historian—to stumble upon "some undiscovered document which will overturn previous generalizations or accepted truths about the past."

As part of his research for a book on the history of women and the family in the United States, he was examining the papers of Dr. Clelia D. Mosher, a dedicated feminist whose long career as professor of personal hygiene at Stanford began in 1893. He had examined rather carefully her correspondence and scrapbooks and was casually glancing at bound volumes of her manuscripts before sending the material back to the stacks.

What followed was described by Dr. Degler in the October 1977 issue of 'Imprint,' published by the Associates of the Stanford University Libraries.

"At first I did not realize the import of what I had in my hands," he wrote. "The first bound volume that I opened contained several hundred sheets covered with printed questions and handwritten answers. When I began to read the questionnaires my excitement quickly mounted. Among the questions which caused my jaw to drop were ones like: 'What is the purpose of intercourse?' 'Is intercourse agreeable to you?' 'How many times do you have intercourse, by week or month?' 'Do you always have a venereal orgasm?' 'Do you use some method of contraception?' 'What methods do you use?' The questions went on for several pages.

"What I had stumbled upon was a survey of sexual practices and attitudes of married women, all of whom had answered the questionnaire in 1920 or before. Since the fertility of white American women fell by 50 percent in the course of the 19th century alone, the methods used to achieve the decline are a central, if troubling question for historians of women and the family. And equally difficult to answer is the question of the character of women's sexual expression and attitudes during those years....

"Perhaps the single most striking aspect of the find was that 70 percent of the women queried were born before 1870. Thus the responses were those of women reared in the nineteenth century.... So far as I know, there is no earlier systematic survey of women's sexual habits than Mosher's."

Professor Degler determined that Dr. Mosher had never published her findings and that apparently no other researcher had made use of them. He judged the material so important that he wrote an article about it for the 'American Historical Review' and has received requests for offprints from places as distant as Poland, Czechoslovakia, and Australia.

Above, left: The materials in the Bender Room of the Department of Special Collections are rare, fragile, intrinsically important, of high esthetic quality, and irreplaceable. The Department of Special Collections began in 1933 with 5,000 volumes; its holdings now number 71,500. Above, right: An unpublished "Interchapter" by John Steinbeck is part of Stanford's Steinbeck Collection, which includes over 1,000 published and unpublished letters and some of his finest early stories in manuscript. Steinbeck attended Stanford on and off during the years 1919 through 1925.

Berkeley involving a coordinated acquisitions policy to prevent unnecessary duplication of expensive books, direct borrowing privileges for faculty and graduate students at both institutions, and intercampus movement of patrons and books. A bus service, called the Gutenberg Express, makes daily round trips between the two campuses.

The cooperative program is one way of offsetting galloping inflation in the price of scholarly materials—a growth rate as much as 10 percent higher than that of the consumer price index. Another is increased emphasis on conservation of materials already on the shelves. Deterioration of books has become a worldwide problem because of the widespread substitution of wood pulp paper for rag paper beginning in the mid-1800s. Books printed on wood pulp paper become too brittle to handle after only about 50 years. Director Weber estimates that between 10 and 20 percent of Stanford's holdings show perceptible deterioration. A conservation officer has been appointed to determine the extent of the deterioration problem and to seek its solution.

For all the emphasis on providing adequate facilities and services and holding down costs, Weber has not lost sight of the fact that it is the quality of the collections that is of first importance. The collection evaluation staff, which includes curators and 30 bibliographers with special area responsibilities, must keep abreast of what is being published in their fields, and they are constantly in touch with deans and faculty members so that they can anticipate curricular and research changes. They must know, for instance, that a new course in European history is in the planning stage and requires a fresh look at Stanford's holdings in that field, or that the appointment of an especially distinguished scientist is pending and calls for substantial upgrading in material on laser technology.

"Stanford, like every other major university, has its unique scholarly personality, so our library collections must be thoughtfully planned and carefully built," Weber observes.

The Faculty

The founding grant empowers the trustees "to employ professors and teachers at the University." But Senator Stanford, accustomed to a strong executive, wrote into the grant that the president of the University alone should have the authority "to remove professors and teachers at will." This power, unchecked and unbalanced, may have been suited to an autocracy, but it was inappropriate to a university. President Eliot of Harvard wrote to Dr. Jordan: "What an extremely disagreeable and inexpedient power of dismissal the Stanfords forced on the president of their University! For all I know, it may work well in a railroad; but it will certainly be extremely inconvenient and injurious in a university."

As to the power of appointment, it was quickly established that the initiative would be with the president, and the trustees would act in confirmation. But the president's power of dismissal, though questioned by some, stood without problems until the notorious case of Edward A. Ross, professor of sociology, came to a head in 1900. Over a period of several years Ross, a stimulating speaker, had been lecturing on and off campus about such subjects as free silver, the purported sins of corporations, and Asian immigrants. Mrs. Stanford considered his positions to be slurs on her husband's name and in violation of the University's nonpartisan stance. Nothing in her background having prepared her for the intricacies of academic freedom, she pressed Dr. Jordan to seek Ross's resignation. Ross complied, then took his case to the newspapers. The furor that ensued was a temporary blow to the University's prestige, but on the positive side it spurred remedy of the basic problem.

First came the long-overdue formal organi-

zation of the professorial staff. The Articles of Organization of the Faculty, worked out by trustee and faculty committees and concurred in by President Jordan, were adopted by the Board of Trustees in 1904. The articles created the Academic Council of assistant, associate, and full professors to give the faculty for the first time a concerted voice in University governance. The articles made clear the supremacy of the council in academic matters, subject to the general authority of the trustees, and established the council's Executive Committee, Advisory Board, and standing committees. In a subsequent resolution, the board decreed that faculty dismissals by the president must be concurred in by the board following consideration and recommendations by the Advisory Board of the Academic Council, steps that still prevail. In view of earlier history, it is interesting to note these words from the preamble to the Statement on Academic Freedom adopted by the faculty and approved by the board in 1974:

"Stanford University's central functions of teaching, learning, research, and scholarship depend upon an atmosphere in which freedom of inquiry, thought, expression, publication and peaceable assembly are given the fullest protection. Expression of the widest range of viewpoints should be encouraged, free from institutional orthodoxy and from internal or external coercion. Further, the holding of appointments at Stanford University should in no way affect faculty members' rights assured by the Constitution of the United States."

By 1968 membership in the Academic Council was approaching a thousand, too large a body to act effectively, and so its small Executive Committee was replaced by a Sen-

ate of 53 representatives elected by the seven schools. Its charter delegates to the Senate the full functions of the council, subject to provisions for review and referendum. In concert with the provost, William F. Miller, the Senate first concentrated on codifying several unwritten and somewhat loosely held faculty policies. These included detailed statements concerning openness in research, faculty discipline, grievance procedures, and academic freedom. More recently the Senate has turned to such matters as the reinstitution of a Western culture requirement for undergraduates and the appointment of women and minority members to the faculty, and has served as a sounding board for University officers as they cope with long-term financial projections.

The Academic Council now numbers approximately 1,200 members, of whom more than half are full professors with tenure. Although rapid strides were made in affirmative action early in the seventies, a disappointingly small number of the faculty are women or members of minority groups. During 1974-79, of 257 appointments or promotions to tenured positions, 20 were women,

One of several letters Mrs. Stanford wrote to Dr. Jordan expressing displeasure with the continued employment of Professor Ross. Mrs. Stanford was a prolific letter writer. Several hundred of her letters, dating from 1876 to 1905, are in the University Archives. Most of them after her husband's death in 1893 are edged in black.

six black, five hispanic, and nine Asian, but these gains were almost entirely offset by retirements, terminations, and resignations. "We need to do more," the provost told the faculty Senate at a recent meeting. The University maintains a supplemental fund to assist departments that turn up especially qualified women or minority candidates for positions not already in their budgets.

For many years the faculty appointment procedure has required that a candidate clear six hurdles, a process that can easily take as long as a year. A recommendation originates in the academic department following a nationwide survey, then is passed in succession to the dean of the school, the provost, the Advisory Board of the Academic Council, the president, and, for confirmation, the Board of Trustees.

The quest is always for the appointee who best combines excellence in both teaching and research. Research can be evaluated in tangibles. There are, for instance, the scholarly honors that are held by the current Stanford faculty. Nine are Nobel Laureates, 11 have won the National Medal of Science, and four the Pulitzer Prize. Ninety-eight are members of the American Academy of Arts and Sciences, and 62 of the National Academy of Sciences.

But teaching ability is harder to pin down. And Stanford, like other major research universities, has often been accused of not putting enough emphasis on teaching in making its faculty appointments and promotions. Yet all of its presidents have maintained that, as President Sterling once said in an address to alumni, "A faculty that is disinterested in what is taught or in effective teaching is not a good faculty."

In 1979 the Senate put into effect a univer-

sal system of student evaluation of teaching as one means of improving instruction and of rating junior faculty for promotion. The system came about gradually in response to quiet but sustained student initiative which attracted faculty support. The evaluation forms cover the professor's presentation, knowledge of subject, course planning, and relationships with students. Videotaping in the classroom, seminars on teaching, and the advice of distinguished retired professors who are members of the Emeriti Undergraduate Council are available to faculty members concerned with their teaching performance.

In addition to their classroom and laboratory duties, faculty members give a lot of time to what might be called good campus citizenship. They serve on an extensive network of administrative committees—there are committees on research, libraries, admissions, even one on parking. Faculty also hold voting membership on committees of the Board of Trustees. They give many hours to academic advising of students, often informally in their living groups, and to faculty "at-homes."

Each year 32 faculty families live in student residences as part of the Resident Fellows Program, which began in 1956. Faculty members are constantly lecturing on the alumni circuit—conferences, day colleges, and other events—and are an integral part of the University's gift-seeking program.

Rating of academic quality is an inexact science at best. But the most recent surveys—taken for the most part among faculty peers across the country—offer a preponderance of evidence as to the distinction of Stanford's professors. They rank the Schools of Education and Business first in the nation, Engineering and Medicine second, and Law third; and they place 17 of the University's departments among the top five in their discipline.

Back in the spring of 1891, when Dr. Jordan was choosing the first teaching staff, he wrote to a friend that Senator Stanford wanted him to hire "no ornamental or idle professors, but a working force," and that still sounds like a fair description of the Stanford faculty.

The Stanford Faculty Club, gift of the Lucie Stern estate, was completed in 1965.

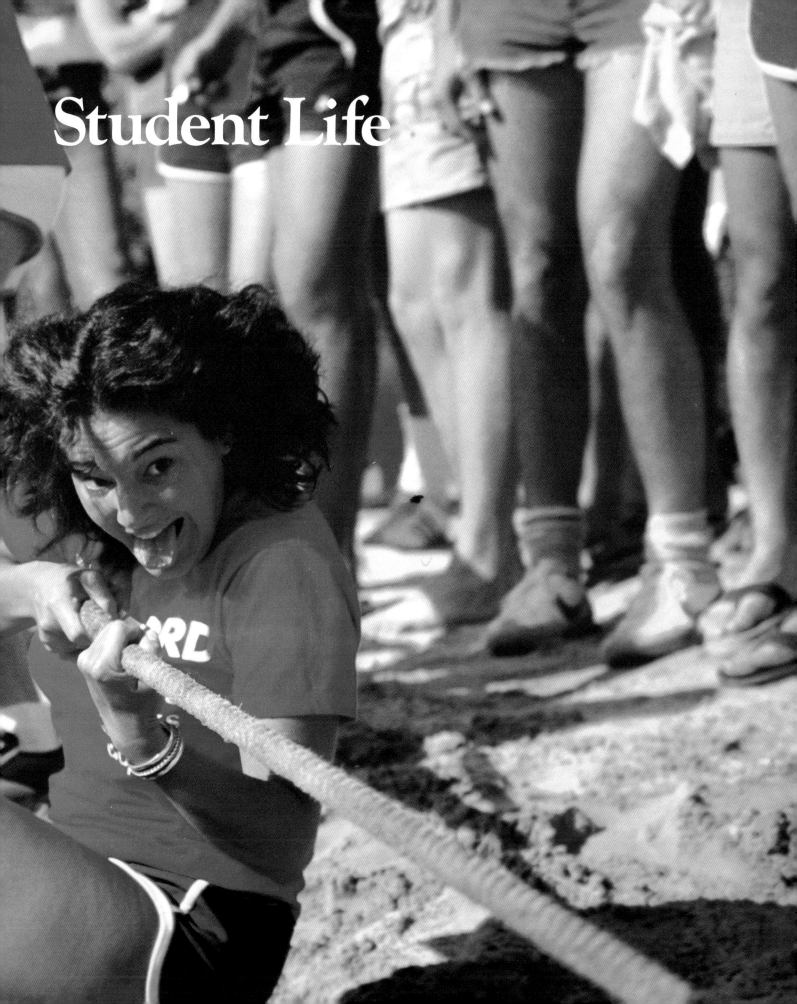

Student Life

The first thing to bear in mind about Stanford students is that they don't fit a stereotype. They are admitted to the University because they are in some way different from the general run, in some way specially talented.

"If we wanted to fill our whole freshman class with kids whose grades ranked them first in their high school classes, we could do it," says Fred Hargadon, dean of admissions, "but that's not our only criterion. We look for some kind of spark, for something that pops out as special."

Each year's 1,500 freshmen are selected from some 11,000 applicants. And once they are on campus the opportunities for self-expression are inescapable. Conformity doesn't have a chance.

"Role and status are not important here," comments James W. Lyons, dean of student affairs. "Talent, independence, and entrepreneurial quality are."

In a recent *Approaching Stanford*, a publication prepared annually by freshmen for the freshman class to follow, there is this admonition: "Don't worry about being unorthodox, because everyone here is different. . . . Above all, be yourself."

The fact that Stanford is a residential university has a strong influence on student life. "Things happen because we are residential,"

Homes away from home: A cozy Encina Hall room at the turn of the century, and parents helping a freshman get settled in Roble Hall. Far left: Old students lend a hand to the new at an Orientation Week square dance. Opposite page: The bookstore draws a crowd at the beginning of the quarter.

Lyons believes. Students govern themselves in their living units. They stage in-house shows, either originals or classics like *The Three-Penny Opera*, and they plan group trips to theater or musical events on campus or in San Francisco. They organize beach and ski outings and recruit teams for intramural competition. They arrange for guest speakers. Some of the halls have student-maintained photography darkrooms and silkscreening and pottery workshops.

Although it is optional after the freshman year, about three-fourths of the undergraduates choose to live on campus. Demand has exceeded supply for the past ten years and shows no signs of abating. An elaborate computerized draw is held each spring to decide who gets to live where the following year.

Four of the smaller houses follow academic themes—La Maison Francaise, La Casa Italiana (which runs a Saturday night pizzeria),

Above: An 1895 painted calfskin wall-hanging with canvas illustration, also painted. Below: Programs from long-ago drama productions. Ram's Head Society, producer of Big Game Gaieties, was founded in 1911 and still offers "original work in the production or interpretation of sketches, songs, musical comedies, and the like."

The Incomparable
Leland Stanford Junior
University Marching
Band, as it is now
known, has evolved
from a traditional
military-style
musical outfit to
a more free-spirited
and zanier group of
musicians. Women
were admitted to the
band's ranks in 1972.

Plug hats (below) forti-fied with many coats of white lead and colorfully decorated were once the distinctive headgear of junior men.

Below: Freshmen once wore beanies, sopho-mores porkpies, and seniors Stetsons. Plug Ugly battles with the sophs (below right), in which the toppers were used as weapons, turned into mayhem and were banned.

The frosh-soph mudfight (far right) was aban-doned in the mid-thirties, some said because the admission of more wom-en was smoothing the fabled Stanford Rough.

Haus Mitteleuropa, and American Studies House—and small classes for credit are also taught in most other residences. Three dormitory wings are organized on cross-cultural ethnic themes for black, Chicano, and Asian-American students. There are freshmanonly dormitories, four-class dormitories, coeducational dormitories, fraternities, eating clubs, and co-op houses where students take turns preparing the meals.

"We'll never be accused of running a cookie-cutter housing program," Dean Lyons observes.

One outcome of the strong residential program is that students nowadays develop an allegiance to their living group and seem to identify more with it than with their class. Advanced placement, stopping-out, and accelerated programs have also lessened class solidarity. There was a time before World War I when every male undergraduate could be identified by his headgear—gray beanies for the freshmen, red felt porkpies for the sophomores, decorated plug hats for the juniors, and for the seniors forest ranger sombreros with class numerals carved in the leather hatband. Frosh-soph mudfights persisted until the late 1930s, the Junior Opera and the Senior Farce were staged, and classes held proms. Now only the senior class holds an election, choosing a council of four presidents rather than a single leader. Class unity

Right: President Jordan may have been startled until he read between the lines of this ingenious poster announcing a student play in the nineties.

BEHOLD! BEWARE STOP! THINK! You will surely need a

DOCTOR

On Thursday, May 24th, 7:30 P. M.

"TO HAVE AND TO LOS

By JOHN SEYMOUR BRISCOE

Greatest Show on Earth this side of the Mississippi and the river

JORDAN

See the Great Street Parade, headed by Doc accompanied by a Chinese lady (not yet found), followed by a FULL Brass Band from Mayfield.

If you come you will certainly be glad and you

WILL WEAR

Your side out laugh when you here Bra Whisker

SEE

THE GREAT PATAGONIAN SCENE
THE HUMAN DOUBLE BOW KNOT
THE ATTACK ON THE BREWERY
The Repulse, the Refusal, Ah! All is

Elegant Costumes, Armor, Top Coats, Pajamas and

BLOOMERS

Will worn with ease

Grace that distinguishes the college-bred man fr car driver   There will be 25 of Palo Alto's cho in line and out.   Free tickets to San Jose give Justice Dyer after the show.

For pure unalloyed fun Tod Walters says he prefers it

IN THE QUAD

reme And that Bell sing

Favorite Song, "Comin Thro the Rye.
See the checkered career of Binks and the striped c Hinks. Hot packages will be handed out at the door

Buy your tickets now and not

TO-MORROW

An me tha Tic

in hand is worth 25c, 50c, and 75c.

Buy your eggs and garden truck at Braccis and the tickets are on sale at Office and the Palace Pharmacy (No dogs and Children admitted)

Press of the Stanley-Taylor

Left: Founded as the Daily Palo Alto in 1891 and still fondly called the "Dippy," The Stanford Daily, housed in Storke Publications Building since 1965, has provided the genesis of many journalistic careers.

Pajamarino paraders, after serenading Roble, headed down Palm Drive to a free show at the Stanford Theater.

at the senior level has shown signs of re-asserting itself in recent years. Seniors have been turning out in overflow crowds for such social events as "happy hours" at the Alpine Inn (formerly Rossotti's) on Alpine Road. The number of graduates choosing to attend commencement nearly doubled in the seventies and baccalaureate had to be moved to the Inner Quad in front of Memorial Church in 1978 to accommodate the crowd.

Stanford enrolls approximately 11,800 students—6,600 undergraduates and 5,200 graduates. Of the undergraduates, some 3,800 are men and 2,800 are women. As an independent institution, the University is free to select its students without constraints of any kind—geographic, religious, ethnic, or sexual. Students come from every state of the Union and from more than 80 foreign countries. Some 15 percent of the undergraduates are Asian-American, black, Chicano, or American Indian.

Because Stanford is privately supported, its charges for tuition and room and board are high—especially so in inflationary times. But this does not mean that only the rich can afford to come. The University's philosophy is that students should select their college for academic reasons, not on the basis of costs. All students who are admitted to undergraduate standing and who qualify for financial aid are offered assistance—either a scholarship, low-interest loan, or part-time work, or a combination of these. About 55 percent of undergraduates qualify for financial aid.

The Associated Students of Stanford University was organized three days after the dedication ceremonies in 1891. The first *Student Handbook*, published in 1892 by the campus YMCA and YWCA, showed that already there were 14 clubs and societies—religious, educational, and social. Today the list tops 200, running, as one campus publication points out, "the gamut from the Hot

The fire whistle, mounted atop the Old Firehouse on Santa Teresa, could be heard all over the campus. Volunteer student firemen, whether in class or not, were expected to count its coded blasts and report posthaste to the scene of the blaze.

FIRE WHISTLES
Leland Stanford Junior University

In case of Fire call up Central, and ask the Operator to ring up the University Power-House, State Name of the House, also the Number indicated on this card for location of Fire.

3	Power House
4	Encina Hall
5	Encina Gym
6	Stanford University Inn
7	Memorial Church
8	History Building
1-2	Library
1-3	Assembly Hall
1-4	Geology Building
1-5	Physics Building
1-6	Roble Hall
2-1	Roble Gym
2-3	Dr. Jordan's Residence
2-4	Chemistry
2-5	Museum
2-6	Stanford Residence
3-1	Postoffice
3-2	Lasuen St. and County Road
3-4	Lasuen Street / County Rd. and Dolores St.
3-5	Salvatierra St. northwest
3-6	Primary School
4-1	Alvarado Row northwest
4-2	Alvarado Row southeast
4-3	San Juan and Dolores Sts.
4-5	Mirada and Dolores Sts.
4-6	Santa Ynez & Reservoir Drive
5-1	Phi Kappa Psi (Cooksey Place)
5-2	Alta Vista
5-3	Stock Farm
5-4	Running Farm (Escondita Cottage)

The big irrigation reservoir on Leland Stanford's farm was quickly adopted by students for water sports. They named it, redundantly, Lake Lagunita. The balcony of the old redwood boathouse (above) collapsed in 1938, pitching spectators into the water. Its replacement still stands.

The first Big Game bonfire was torched in 1898, the last in 1977, when ecological and public safety arguments prevailed.

The four little professors marched across Chappie's pages in postwar years.

196

Chaparral, *Stanford's humor magazine, first appeared in October 1899, and with only a few absences it has survived the years. Its jester-like mascot continues to symbolize its "Old Boy" editor.*

Air Balloon Club to Stanford College Republicans." A student observes, "You have to work pretty hard to be bored at Stanford. Almost anything you want to do here you can find some club, team, organization, or friend to do it with." The members of several organizations work as volunteers in surrounding cities or tutor in local schools.

Complete freedom for students to control their own affairs was professed early in the life of the University, but there were continuing skirmishes between student and adult authority until the right of student self-government was formally promulgated in 1912. "They did well," recounts Registrar Mitchell. "It was not always easy, they stumbled occasionally, but they had valuable experience."

In 1921 1,700 students, nearly three-fourths of the student body, petitioned President Wilbur that responsibility for the conduct of examinations be granted to the students, and the Academic Council gave its approval. This was the beginning of the Stanford Honor Code and since that day examinations have not been proctored. As it is formulated today, the Honor Code covers honesty in all academic work, not just exams, and obligates students to see that others, as well as themselves, observe its conditions.

"The Honor Code works because it mirrors the dominant values at Stanford," declares Dean Lyons. "When students come here they turn on their radar to see if the campus behaves like we say it does. They are relieved to see that they can be honest in their work here without suffering disadvantage. There is nothing more important than this to the enterprise of learning, for, after all, knowledge must rest on a base of honesty and trust."

Student residences, clockwise from left: Robert S. Moore, South (American Studies); Hammarskjold House, where foreign students gather; Robert S. Moore, North (La Casa Italiana); Grove-Lasuen, once a faculty duplex.

PATH OF BRONZE

The class of '96 was the first to think of imbedding a bronze plate, with class numerals and borders worked in gray babbit metal, into a square of the walk in front of Memorial Church. That is why theirs sits squarely in front of the center door to the church—a fortuitous circumstance, class members pointed out, because '96 reads the same in both directions.

Every class since has added its plate, with an airtight metal box enclosing memorabilia sealed beneath it, in a ceremony at commencement time, and the classes earlier than '96 eventually added theirs. The pioneer class of '95, the first to complete the full four years and never happy to be second in anything, slipped theirs in late one evening in 1903, according to the 'Alumnus,' "without public announcement or alien witness."

David Starr Jordan, in accepting the '97 plate, announced that he had stepped off the squares in the concrete walk around the Inner Quad and that "when the fair year of 2517 comes, we shall find ourselves at this point again."

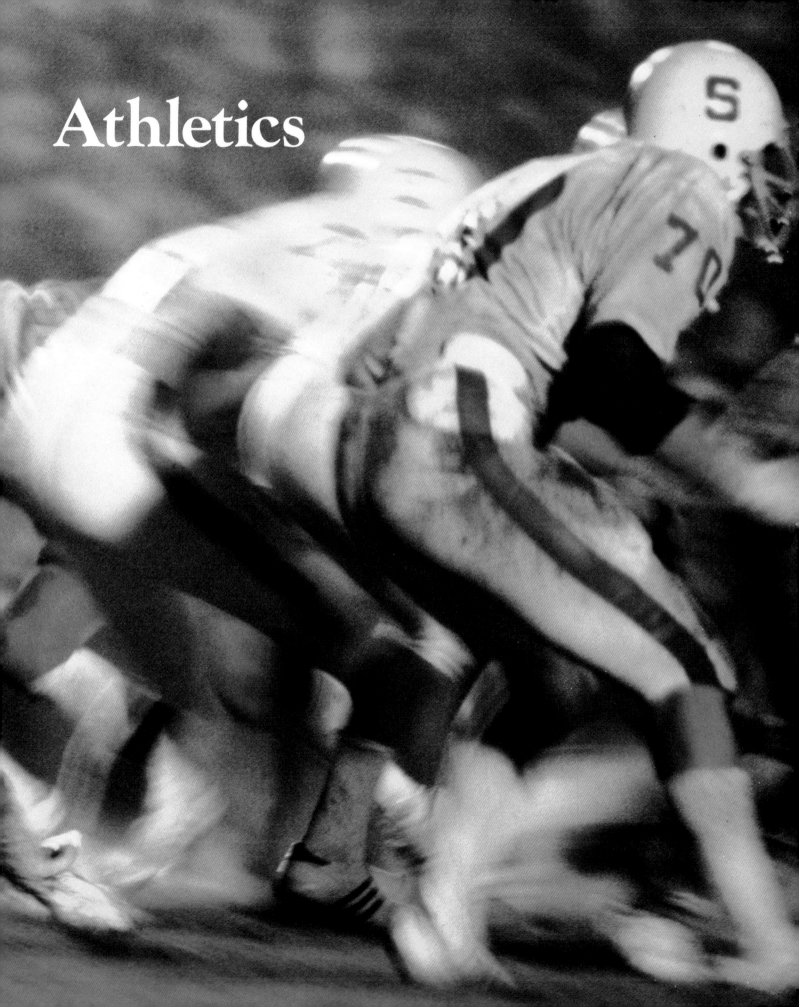

Athletics

Very few people, other than the dyed-in-the-Cardinal sports fans of earlier generations, remember the late Harry Maloney. And that is unfortunate because, more than three decades after his retirement from coaching, the influence of this rugged, likable Irishman's philosophy on the Stanford approach to athletics is still very strong.

Harry came to Stanford in 1908 and retired 36 years later. During most of those years he coached soccer, fencing, and boxing and for shorter periods track and field, wrestling, and rugby—not to mention a period as trainer. When the Harry Maloney Field for soccer was dedicated, President Wilbur insisted that the full name be used "because there are many Maloneys but only one *Harry* Maloney." What he meant was that, in addition to being an excellent coach, Harry was equally concerned that Stanford turn out men and women who enjoyed games while learning the values of teamwork, individual development, and especially how to win or lose graciously.

When someone, especially a teacher, holds fast to ideals as long and as forcefully as Harry Maloney did, the imprint lasts. "Stanford considers athletics to be an integral part of a full and rewarding life," says Andy Geiger, who was appointed the University's fourth director of athletics in 1979. "The athlete learns that true discipline comes from within. And once learned, the lesson carries over into one's studies, one's career, one's whole life."

Opposite: The Stanford Axe, brandished in accompaniment to the rousing "Give 'em the Axe" yell, was stolen by Cal rooters at an 1896 baseball game.

Recaptured by Stanford's "Immortal 21" in a daring raid in 1930, the Axe is now the trophy of the Big Game.

Above: Harry Maloney. Right: "The BAC," headquarters of Stanford athletics. Below: Excursion ticket to the first Big Game at the Haight Street ballpark in San Francisco.

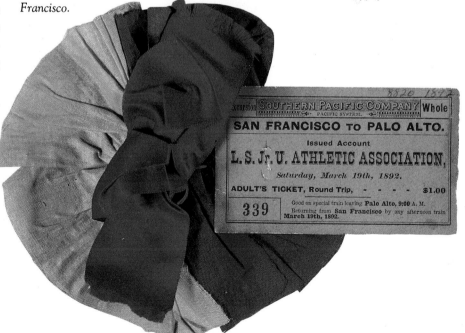

202

Football legends of the mid-twenties: Ernie Nevers, all-time All-America fullback, and Glenn S. "Pop" Warner, coaching wizard. Both are in the National Football Hall of Fame. Below: The "Vow Boys" block perfectly to open a path for Bobby Grayson in the 1935 Big Game. Stanford won, 20-6.

Bottom: Tom Williams, later to be a prominent Palo Alto physician and an original member of the old Board of Ath- *letic Control, played center on the '95 and '96 varsities. His football gear is in the University Archives.*

The 1930 Big Game ball. Legible signatures include those of Pop Warner, Captain Ray Tandy, Phil Moffatt, and Harlow Rothert.

203

Stanford people, whether novice or skilled, have always had an open invitation to use the University's athletic facilities and try out for teams. This has led to an unusually broad program. A unified Department of Athletics, Physical Education, and Recreation, under which the men's and women's programs were joined in 1975, supervises:

- Intercollegiate competition in 13 men's and 10 women's varsity sports, with 560 participants.
- Club sports—24 teams and 1,200 participants in extramural competition.
- Intramurals—10,000 participants in 20 sports.
- Physical education classes with enrollment of 9,000.
- Recreation—jogging, tennis, swimming, frisbee tossing, or whatever by an uncounted but huge number of students, faculty, staff, and family members.

The oratory of Stanford's dedication in the fall of '91 had scarcely died away before a hardy band of freshmen and a few transfers were practicing football on a baked adobe stubble field east of Encina Hall. Soon they acquired a coach in the person of an assistant professor of English whose previous experience had been in rugby. The University of California team, which had already established quite a reputation, called them "Jordan's Schoolboys"—that is, they did until Stanford beat them 14 to 10 in the first Big Game, played in March of 1892 in a San Francisco ballpark. Thus began Stanford's participation in intercollegiate competition, and in particular the intense rivalry that exists with Berkeley in all sports, epitomized by the annual struggle in the Big Game for the Stanford Axe.

Big Game programs of various vintages. The use of the Indian as a mascot for Stanford athletic teams, begun in the early 1930s, was discontinued in 1971.

It would take a book to chronicle all of the high points of Stanford's athletic history. (As a matter of fact, there is such a book, *The Color of Life is Red*, by Don Liebendorfer. In 1924, Don, a Stanford senior, became sports publicity director, a job he held for 45 years.) But these few special events should be cited, even at the risk of overlooking many more:

- Glenn S. "Pop" Warner arriving on the Farm in 1924 to outfox opponents with his new double-wing attack; his fullback, Ernie Nevers, plunging to all-time All-America honors.

- Ben Eastman—"Blazin' Ben," Dink Templeton's greatest runner—setting world records in the 440 and 880 one week apart in 1932.

- The "Vow Boys" of 1933-35 redeeming their pledge never to lose to USC, holding opponents to an average of 3 points in 31 games, going to the Rose Bowl three straight years.

- Angelo "Hank" Luisetti electrifying 17,000 fans in Madison Square Garden with his running one-handed basketball shots; John Bunn's squad introducing modern, fast-break basketball that night in 1936 as they left a favored Long Island U. team flat-footed.

- Marjorie Gestring, diver, and Brenda Helser, freestyle swimmer—both Olympic gold medal winners—outclassing their competition in the thirties and forties; Linda Jezek setting a world's backstroke record in 1979.

- The 1940 "Wow Boys," tutored by Clark Shaughnessy, revolutionizing football with a retooled T-formation and, in Frank Albert, starting a long line of superlative passing quarterbacks.

- Bob Mathias becoming, in 1952, the only athlete to play in the Rose Bowl and win an Olympic gold medal in the same year.

- Chuck Essegian rocketing eight home runs out of the Sunken Diamond in the 1952 season, before the fences were shortened by an average of 45 feet.

- Winning back-to-back Rose Bowl games in 1971 and 1972 over highly favored Ohio State and Michigan; Rod Garcia kicking a 31-yard field goal with 12 seconds to go to win the Michigan game.

- Tennis teams capturing four national championships in the 1970s, capped in 1978 by victories by both the men's and the women's teams, and in 1979 by Kathy Jordan's becoming the first player in women's collegiate tennis history to win the national title in both singles and doubles.

Above, left: Under gathering storm clouds and fading sunlight, two Stanford crews train on Lake Washington near Seattle for the 1956 Olympics at Melbourne. Both teams won gold medals. Left to right, the pair is Jim Fifer and Duvall Hecht and the pair-with-coxswain, Dan Ayrault, Conn Findlay, and Kurt Seiffert.

Opposite: Kimberly Belton, '80, a four-year starter on the Stanford basketball team, became Stanford's all-time scorer (1,615 points), all-time rebounder (955 rebounds), and best career field goal shooter (57.2%). He was one of 16 players nationwide to receive an NCAA postgraduate scholarship.

Stanford fields 13 men's and 10 women's varsity sports teams, while thousands of other students participate in 24 club sports and 20 intramural sports.

Since the era of graduate student managers ended in 1924, Stanford athletics have been directed by only four men. The first was Alfred R. (Al) Masters, who held the post for 38 years and was one of the most distinguished sports administrators in college history. He was succeeded in 1963 by Charles A. (Chuck) Taylor, All-America guard with the Wow Boys in 1941 and Coach of the Year with his 1951 Stanford Rose Bowl team. Joseph H. (Joe) Ruetz took over in 1972, guiding the merger of the men's and women's departments and expansion of women's intercollegiate competition. He retired in 1979.

"Stanford is recognized by colleges and universities across the country for its determination to combine an excellent academic program with an excellent athletic program," the current director, Andy Geiger, declares. "There is no shortage of outstanding athletes who are also outstanding students. We simply have to look for them, talk to them about subjects other than sports, and offer them programs of high quality in the fields in which they want to study. In short, we have to be interested in the whole person, and we are."

Left: Robert L. "Dink" Templeton at Angell Field with Gus Meier, world-record hurdler. Dink's teams placed, first, second, or third in the NCAA meet in seven of his 18 years (1921-39) as head track coach. Right: Payton Jordan, track and field coach for 22 years (1957-79), is a world champion in senior sprint events. He was coach of the 1968 Olympic team.

Above: A class in aikido. Stanford students may take courses in five different martial arts, all of which include readings in the philosophy of the art as well as the development of physical skills.

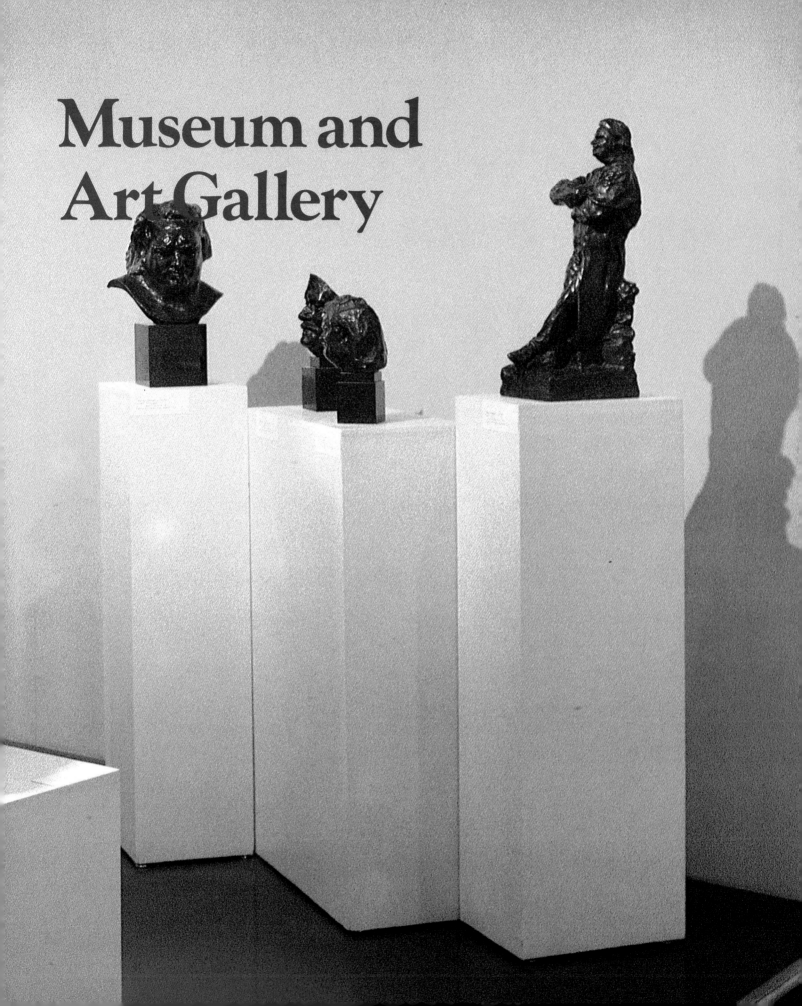

Museum and
Art Gallery

Leland Stanford Jr., at 15, was already an avid and knowledgeable collector of Egyptian bronzes, Greek vases, and other items of archaeological importance. He had confided to his parents that someday he hoped to build a museum in California modeled after the neoclassical National Museum of Athens, which he had visited.

When it came time to build a memorial to their son, Senator and Mrs. Stanford decided to build not just a museum but a complete university. Still, they retained a special sentimental attachment to the idea of a museum and the Senator set aside a sum of money in his wife's name and said that all decisions in the design and construction of the University's museum would be hers. Determined that the architecture would follow the wish of her son, Mrs. Stanford eased the building out of architect Coolidge's plans for the Romanesque quadrangles onto a site of its own in the direction of the Arboretum. She commissioned George Percy, a San Francisco architect and family friend, to design a building closely resembling the Athens museum.

It was already late in 1890 and Mrs. Stanford wanted the Leland Stanford Junior Museum to be ready when classes were to begin a year later, so the bold decision was made to use the new technique of reinforced concrete construction. Ernest Ransome, a major contributor to modern concrete technology, was engaged as engineer, and the building incorporates a number of his innovations, such as reinforcing bars twisted to prevent slippage (an idea that was said to have come to him while he was idly twisting a rubber band) and tool-dressed surfaces to show the texture of the aggregate. A historian of architecture has written of the Stanford museum: "For the first time, con-

crete was considered to be the concern of skilled craftsmen, and capable of displaying an inherent beauty."

Young Leland's collections, along with family memorabilia and works of art the Stanfords had purchased for their various residences, were placed in the museum. Mrs. Stanford gained permission to open the great Baron Ikeda collection while it waited on the San Francisco docks en route from Japan to London for sale—and parts of it went to Stanford instead. She was the "unknown millionaire from the West" who outbid the Boston Museum for a portion of the Cesnola collection of classical antiquities from Cyprus, and she acquired Egyptian material through discerning support of the Egyptian Exploration Society.

After funds from her husband's estate became available in 1898, Mrs. Stanford added three wings to the museum, enclosing a quadrangle. These were not so well built as the original portion and in the 1906 earthquake

Museum-goers and a fifth-century B.C. urn.

Opposite: The vaulting entrance rotunda of the Stanford Museum of Art. Mrs. Stanford spent the last days of her life enlarging and placing the collections in this building, which was her special memorial to her son.

Top: A marble Greek casts an appraising eye at Arnaldo Pomodoro's The Cube. Middle: The Stanford Museum owns one of the nation's most important collections of the works of sculptor Auguste Rodin, the gift of the B. Gerald Cantor Foundation.

the two side wings were irreparably damaged and the back wing was reduced from two stories to one, eventually to be occupied by the Anatomy and Bacteriology Departments of the Medical School.

The original building came through almost unscathed but the collections were badly damaged—shaken, Jordan said, "like peas in a pod." The museum was reopened on a limited basis in 1909, but, having lost its patron when Mrs. Stanford died in 1905, it languished. It was finally closed to the public in 1945, and reopened in 1954 after some improvement, but its real renaissance began when Lorenz Eitner was appointed chairman of the Department of Art and director of the museum and art gallery in 1963. It is now a respected institution with multistrengths in its permanent collections, special exhibitions, academic and research programs, community-oriented educational services, and lecture and publication programs.

"Frugal as our expenditures have always had to be, we are still one of the most acquisitive museums in the Bay Area," Eitner comments. The museum adds between 300 and 400 items a year. It has strong collections in European art of the eighteenth and nineteenth centuries; Oriental art, including the outstanding Frank E. Buck Jade Collection; Southwest American Indian artifacts; the sculpture of Rodin, thanks to the generosity of B. Gerald Cantor; and the history of photography, occasioned by the work of Eadweard Muybridge at the Palo Alto Stock Farm in the nineteenth century. The art of Egypt and Greece are well represented. The Stanford Room is devoted to the lives of the University founders and their son.

All acquisitions are the result of private benefactions—rather than from University

Mosaics on the facade of the Museum were executed by the Salviati Studios of Venice, the same firm which designed and placed the mosaics in Memorial Church.

215

general funds—either from individuals, foundations, or as a result of the devoted labor of the 1,500 families who belong to the Committee for Art at Stanford. Among the committee's activities is a biennial Treasure Mart, a sale of donated art objects, furniture, jewelry, and other items. A recent mart added $175,000 to the museum's purchase funds.

The museum staff puts together some 25 major exhibitions a year, mounting them in the Sarah Love Miedel Room or the Marie Stauffer Sigall Gallery in the museum or in the separate Thomas Welton Stanford Art Gallery. Thomas, a younger brother of Leland, started his fortune by taking a cargo of coal oil and lamps to Australia. After weeks

Above: The Thomas Welton Stanford Art Gallery. Below: The Stanford Museum of Art.

of desperate seasickness, he arrived in Melbourne and vowed never to put to sea again. In 1911 he sent the University funds for building the art gallery. It was to have been the northwest corner of a new, arcaded quadrangle, of which the Main Library was also to have become a part, but this grand design was not carried out.

Academic use of the museum is of primary importance. Art classes are held there and graduate students and faculty use its collections for research. "The museum is to the art researcher what the physics lab is to the physicist, except that we don't smash things," the director says. "Building a museum is as important for a university as building a library."

"For Ages to Come..."

Frank Lloyd Wright, when he strolled through the Stanford quadrangles in 1936, remarked that they represented the greatest university architecture of his knowledge and that they revealed "the hand of the master"—by which, art historian Paul Turner interprets, Wright meant Henry Hobson Richardson.

The rehabilitation of the fine old buildings of the original Quads has become the major segment of the University's building program, not simply to preserve a priceless architectural heritage but also because they have not outlived their purpose. They are still the University's "inner city."

Except for repair of damage done by the 1906 earthquake and the minimum-cost conversion of the old Assembly Hall into Business School quarters, the Quad buildings were untouched for 40 years. The complete remodeling of an Inner Quad building for the president's office occurred in 1944 and most of the one-story buildings have since been modernized and double-decked on the inside. The first interior reconstruction of a multistory Outer Quad building, including the strengthening of the walls against earthquake hazard, was completed in 1950. This was the conversion of the old Administration Building into Law School quarters. During the construction boom of the next two decades the emphasis was on new buildings spotted in widening circles outside the old Quads, although Physics Corner on the Outer Quad was converted to the Alfred P. Sloan Mathematics Center in 1964.

A new decade brought even more stringent earthquake safety standards and the University began rebuilding the interiors of the major Outer Quad structures as fast as funds became available. Jordan Hall has been re-

done for the Psychology Department; the old Physiology Building, renamed Margaret Jacks Hall, is the home of the Computer Science Department and the Boys Town Center for Youth Development; and History Corner, where it was possible to retain the old wrought steel stair railings and to recreate the original woodwork in naturally finished red oak, has been reconstructed for the History Department. Building 120 at the corner of Memorial Court is scheduled to be ready in 1982 for the Department of Communication and the Department of Sociology. Its original skylight will be reopened to illuminate a four-story central atrium.

Restoration of these buildings without changing their outside handsomeness is an expensive business—about 30 percent more costly than new construction. The interior must be gutted and the roof removed —only the outer walls of unreinforced masonry remain. A framework of concrete and steel is erected inside. The interior surfaces of the old walls are then coated with 6 to 12 inches of gunite concrete and concrete floors are poured. Old and new become a monolith.

What makes it all worthwhile is that these buildings of sandstone and tile are invested with a new inner strength, efficiency, and airiness that fit them to continue for many more decades as the academic heart of the University. Thus modern technology promises fulfillment of Jane Stanford's fondest wish. "These noble buildings," she wrote shortly before her death, "are not alone for the present but for ages to come, when generation after generation has passed and gone, and when, I hope and pray, these buildings will stand and serve the purpose for which they were erected, namely, for the benefit of the young of our land."

Chronology

1824–*March 9*—Birth of Leland Stanford (now celebrated as Founders' Day)

1828–*August 25*—Birth of Jane Lathrop Stanford

1868–*May 14*—Birth of Leland Stanford Junior

1876–First purchase of Palo Alto Farm land by Leland Stanford

1884–*March 13*—Death of Leland Stanford Junior

1885–*November 11*—Founding Grant executed

1885–*November 14*—First meeting of Board of Trustees

1887–*May 14*—Cornerstone of University laid

1891–*March 22*—David Starr Jordan appointed first president of University

1891–*October 1*—University opened with 12 departments, 465 students, and 15 faculty members

1891–Associated Students of Stanford University (ASSU) organized

1892–*March 19*—First Big Game, played in San Francisco, won by Stanford 14-10

1892–*June 15*—Stanford Alumni Association organized

1892–*June 27*—Hopkins Seaside Laboratory (later named Hopkins Marine Station) opened

1893–*June 21*—Death of Leland Stanford

1896–*March 2*—Government suit against Stanford estate dismissed

1900–Undergraduate enrollment 1,119; graduate enrollment 117; faculty 75

1903–*June 1*—Jane Stanford turns over powers as surviving founder to Board of Trustees

1903–*July 6*—Jane Stanford elected president of trustees

1904–Academic Council of full, associate, and assistant professors organized

1905–*February 28*—Death of Jane Stanford

1906–*April 18*—Earthquake destroys portion of campus

1908–*October 30*—Transfer of Cooper Medical College to University

1908–Department of Law changed to School of Law

1910–Undergraduate enrollment 1,358; graduate enrollment 157; Academic Council members 112

1912–ASSU accepts responsibility for student personal conduct under Fundamental Standard

1913–*May 20*—John Casper Branner appointed second president

1913–*May 23*—David Starr Jordan appointed first chancellor

1913–Ray Lyman Wilbur appointed dean of School of Medicine

1916–*January 1*—Ray Lyman Wilbur becomes third president

1916–William Ophüls appointed dean of School of Medicine

1916–Charles Andrews Huston appointed dean of Law School

1917–Department of Education changed to School of Education; Ellwood P. Cubberley appointed dean

1920–Undergraduate enrollment 2,165; graduate enrollment 283; Academic Council members 150

1920–*January 1*—Tuition fee introduced

1920–*June 17*—Stanford Home for Convalescent Children dedicated

1921–Honor Code covering academic work adopted

1922–*March 1*—Death of President Emeritus Branner

1923–Marion Rice Kirkwood appointed dean of Law School

1925–School of Engineering organized; Theodore J. Hoover appointed dean

1925–Graduate School of Business opened; Willard Eugene Hotchkiss appointed dean

1930–Undergraduate enrollment 2,706; graduate enrollment 893; Academic Council members 271

1931–*September 19*—Death of Chancellor Emeritus Jordan

1931–J. Hugh Jackson appointed dean of Graduate School of Business

1933–*May 11*—"500" limit on women students removed

1933–Loren Roscoe Chandler appointed dean of School of Medicine

1934–Grayson N. Kefauver appointed dean of School of Education

1936–Samuel B. Morris appointed dean of School of Engineering

1940–Undergraduate enrollment 3,218; graduate enrollment 1,146; Academic Council members 309

1942–*January 1*—Ray Lyman Wilbur becomes chancellor

1943–*January 21*—Donald Bertrand Tresidder appointed fourth president

1944–*April 20*—Trustees discontinue sororities

1946–Frederick E. Terman appointed dean of School of Engineering

1946–A. John Bartky appointed dean of School of Education

1947–School of Mineral Sciences (later named Earth Sciences) organized; A. Irving Levorsen appointed dean

1947–Carl B. Spaeth appointed dean of Law School

1948–*January 28*—Death of President Donald B. Tresidder

1948–Schools of Biological Sciences, Humanities, Physical Sciences, and Social Sciences merged into School of Humanities and Sciences; Clarence H. Faust appointed dean

1949–*April 1*—J.E. Wallace Sterling becomes fifth president

1949–*June 26*—Death of Chancellor Ray Lyman Wilbur

1950–Undergraduate enrollment 4,794; graduate enrollment 2,841; Academic Council members 372

1950–Charles F. Park Jr. appointed dean of School of Mineral Sciences

1951–Douglas M. Whitaker appointed dean of School of Humanities and Sciences

1952–*April 1*—Douglas M. Whitaker becomes first provost

1953–Windsor C. Cutting appointed dean of School of Medicine

1954–I. James Quillen appointed dean of School of Education

1955–Frederick E. Terman becomes provost (title changed to vice-president and provost in 1959)

1956–Philip H. Rhinelander appointed dean of School of Humanities and Sciences

1958–First campus of Overseas Studies Program opened near Stuttgart, Germany

1958–Ernest C. Arbuckle appointed dean of Graduate School of Business

1958–Robert H. Alway appointed dean of School of Medicine

1958–Joseph M. Pettit appointed dean of School of Engineering

1958–Alf E. Brandin appointed vice-president for business affairs

1959–Kenneth M. Cuthbertson appointed vice-president for finance (later vice-president for development)

1959–*September*—Medical School's move from San Francisco to campus completed

1960–Undergraduate enrollment 5,603; graduate enrollment 3,636; Academic Council members 619

1961–Robert R. Sears appointed dean of School of Humanities and Sciences

1964–*April*—Three-year PACE fund drive completed; $113 million raised

1964–Bayless A. Manning appointed dean of Law School

1965–Robert J. Glaser appointed vice-president for medical affairs and dean of School of Medicine

1965–Richard H. Jahns appointed dean of School of Earth Sciences

1966–H. Thomas James appointed dean of School of Education

1966–Stanford Linear Accelerator Center begins operation

1967–Richard W. Lyman appointed vice-president and provost

1968–*September 1*—J.E. Wallace Sterling becomes chancellor

1968–*September 12*—Inaugural session of Senate of Academic Council held

1968–*December 1*—Kenneth S. Pitzer becomes sixth president

1969–Two-year Study of Education at Stanford completed

1969–Arjay Miller appointed dean of Graduate School of Business

1970–Undergraduate enrollment 6,303; graduate enrollment 5,159; Academic Council members 1,029

1970–*September 24*—Richard W. Lyman becomes seventh president

1970–Albert H. Hastorf appointed dean of School of Humanities and Sciences

1971–William F. Miller appointed vice-president and provost

1971–Robert R. Augsburger appointed vice-president for business and finance

1971–Clayton Rich appointed vice-president for medical affairs and dean of the School of Medicine

1971–Arthur A. Coladarci appointed dean of School of Education

1971–Thomas Ehrlich appointed dean of Law School

1972–William M. Kays appointed dean of School of Engineering

1973–Halsey L. Royden appointed dean of School of Humanities and Sciences

1974–Robert M. Rosenzweig appointed vice-president for public affairs

1976–Charles J. Meyers appointed dean of Law School

1977–*May 1*—Five-year Campaign for Stanford completed; $304 million raised

1977–William F. Massy appointed vice-president for business and finance

1977–Joel P. Smith appointed vice-president for development

1979–Undergraduate enrollment 6,638; graduate enrollment 5,227; Academic Council members 1,218

1979–Donald Kennedy appointed vice-president and provost

1979–Allan V. Cox appointed dean of School of Earth Sciences

1979–J. Myron Atkin appointed dean of School of Education

1980–Rene C. McPherson appointed dean of Graduate School of Business

1980–*June 13*—Donald Kennedy appointed eighth president

Bibliography

222

The list that follows gives the principal written sources for *Stanford: From the Foothills to the Bay.* It leaves uncited a multitude of letters, papers, scrapbooks, newspaper clippings, magazine articles, informal reminiscences such as those of Mrs. David Starr Jordan and Mrs. John Casper Branner, and other sources—all of which contributed much to the story.

Allen, Peter C. "Stanford from the Beginning." Stanford, California: Stanford University, 1978.

————. "Stanford University: An Academic 'Inner City.'" In *Historic Preservation.* Washington, D.C.: National Trust for Historic Preservation, April-June 1978.

Bancroft, Hubert Howe. *History of the Life of Leland Stanford.* Oakland, California: Biobooks, 1952.

Berner, Bertha. *Mrs. Leland Stanford: An Intimate Account.* Stanford, California: Stanford University Press, 1935.

Clark, George T. *Leland Stanford: War Governor of California, Railroad Builder, and Founder of Stanford University.* Stanford, California: Stanford University Press, 1931.

Dupen, Douglas W. *The Story of Stanford's Two-Mile-Long Accelerator.* Menlo Park, California: Stanford Linear Accelerator Center, 1966.

Elliott, Ellen Coit. *It Happened This Way.* Stanford, California: Stanford University Press, 1940.

Elliott, Orrin Leslie. *Stanford University: The First Twenty-five Years.* Stanford, California: Stanford University Press, 1937.

Hoover, Herbert. *The Memoirs of Herbert Hoover: Years of Adventure, 1874-1920.* New York: Macmillan Company, 1951.

Howard, Arthur David. *Evolution of the Landscape of the San Francisco Bay Region.* Berkeley: University of California Press, 1962.

Jordan, David Starr. *The Days of a Man: Being Memories of a Naturalist, Teacher and Minor Prophet of Democracy.* World Book Company, 1922.

Liebendorfer, Don E. *The Color of Life Is Red: A History of Stanford Athletics, 1892-1972.* Stanford, California: Department of Athletics, Stanford University, 1972.

Mirrielees, Edith R., ed. *Stanford Mosaic: Reminiscences of the First Seventy Years at Stanford University.* Stanford, California: Stanford University, 1962.

Mitchell, J. Pearce. *Stanford University: 1916-1941.* Stanford, California: Stanford University, 1958.

Nagel, Gunther W. *Jane Stanford: Her Life and Letters.* Stanford, California: Stanford Alumni Association, 1975.

Nash, Herbert C. *In Memoriam: Leland Stanford, Jr.* Privately published, 1884.

Snyder, Bill. "Hopkins Marine Station." In *The Stanford Magazine,* Fall/Winter 1977, pp. 4-13.

The Stanford Business School Alumni Bulletin, Fiftieth Anniversary Issue, Spring 1975.

Treutlein, Theodore E. *San Francisco Bay: Discovery and Colonization, 1769-1776.* San Francisco: California Historical Society, 1968.

Turner, Paul V; Vetrocq, Marcia E.; and Weitze, Karen. *The Founders and the Architects: The Design of Stanford University.* Stanford, California: Department of Art, Stanford University, 1976.

Walsh, John. "Stanford's Search for Solutions." In *Academic Transformation: Seventeen Institutions under Pressure,* edited by David Riesman and Verne A. Stadtman. New York: McGraw-Hill Book Company, 1973.

Weymouth, Alice Jenkins. "The Palo Alto Tree." Stanford, California: Stanford University Press, 1930.

Wilbur, Ray Lyman. *The Memoirs of Ray Lyman Wilbur: 1875-1949.* Stanford, California: Stanford University Press, 1960.

Building Inventory

Building Inventory

(The numbering corresponds to numbering on the maps, pages 44 and 74-75. Architects' names are given in parentheses. Uses listed are *former* uses; for *current* uses, see the keys to maps.)

Inner Quad

Inner Quad academic and office buildings were designed by Shepley, Rutan & Coolidge and were completed in 1891. Memorial Church was designed by Shepley, Rutan & Coolidge, modified by Clinton Day, and was completed in 1902.

1. **Building 1**
   Remodeled 1950 and 1956 (Spencer and Ambrose). University Library; Law; Placement Service; University Relations; Academic Planning

2. **Building 10**
   Remodeled 1944 (Spencer and Ambrose) and 1956 (Spencer, Lee and Busse). Mathematics; Law

3. **Building 20**
   Remodeled 1957 (Spencer and Lee). English; Education; Greek; Latin; Political Science

4. **Building 30**
   Greek; Latin; German; English; Food Research Institute

5. **Building 40**
   Remodeled 1960 (Spencer and Lee). Botany; Romance Languages; Applied Mathematics; Philosophy; Education

6. **Building 50**
   Remodeled 1956 (Spencer and Ambrose). Physics; Education; Humanities

7. **Stanford Memorial Church**

8. **Building 60** (contains original cornerstone) Remodeled 1958 (Spencer and Lee). Chemistry; Hygiene; Metallurgy; Applied Mathematics; Mathematics

9. **Building 70**
   Remodeled 1958 (Spencer and Lee). Chemistry; Metallurgy; Mathematics

10. **Building 80**
    Zoology; Ombudsman

11. **Building 90**
    Remodeled 1959 (Spencer and Lee). Physiology; Hygiene; Art

12. **Building 100**
    Remodeled 1950 (Spencer and Ambrose). University chapel; Administration

13. **Building 110**
    Remodeled 1950 (Spencer and Ambrose) and 1968 (Spencer, Lee and Busse). President; Registrar; German; Law School

Outer Quad

All Outer Quad buildings were originally designed by Shepley, Rutan & Coolidge; plans for some of these buildings were modified by other architects.

14. **Building 120**
    Completed 1898 (modified by Clinton Day); remodeled 1937 (Bakewell and Brown); remodeling scheduled for completion 1982 (Esherick, Homsey, Dodge and Davis). Assembly Hall; Business School; Affirmative Action; University Relations

15. **Building 160**
    Completed 1900 (modified by Clinton Day); remodeled 1950 (Weihe, Frick and Kruse). Thomas Welton Stanford Library; President; Controller; Financial Vice-President; Registrar; Alumni Association; General Secretary; Law School

16. **Building 170**
    Completed 1900; remodeled 1964 (M.T. Pflueger). Thomas Welton Stanford Library (stacks); Administration; Law Annex; History

17. **Building 200**
    (History Corner; formerly also English Corner) Completed 1903 (modified by Charles E. Hodges); remodeled 1979 (Stone, Marraccini and Patterson/Esherick, Homsey, Dodge and Davis). Economics; English; Sociology

18. **Building 240**
    Completed 1898; remodeled 1957 (Spencer and Lee). Romanic Languages; Comparative Literature

19. **Building 250**
    Completed 1898; remodeled 1958 (Spencer and Lee). Treasurer; Business Office; Classics; International Relations

20. **Building 260**
    (Engineering Corner) Completed 1904 (modified by Charles E. Hodges). Engineering

21. **Building 300**
    Completed ca. 1904. Engineering Draughting; Electrical Engineering Laboratory; General Secretary; Alumni Association; Civil Engineering

22. **Building 310**
    Completed 1906. Drawing and Painting; Graphic Arts; Art and Architecture

23. **Building 320**
    (Geology Corner) Completed 1906 (modified by Charles E. Hodges). Geology and Mining

24. **Building 360**
    Completed 1906. Mineralogy

25. **Building 370**
    Completed 1903 (modified by Charles E. Hodges); remodeled 1949 (Spencer and Ambrose). Mineral Sciences; Physics

26. **Building 380**
    (Alfred P. Sloan Mathematics Corner; formerly Physics Corner) Completed 1903 (modified by Clinton Day); remodeled 1964 (Spencer, Lee and Busse). Philosophy; Physics; Psychology

27. **Building 420**
    (Jordan Hall) Completed 1903 (modified by Clinton Day); remodeled 1970 (Spencer, Lee and Busse)

28. **Building 460**
    (Margaret Jacks Hall) Completed 1903 (modified by Clinton Day); remodeled 1979 (Spencer Associates). Physiology; Botany; Center for Research in International Studies

Buildings outside Quad

1. **Cowell Student Health Center**
   Completed 1967 (Ernest J. Kump Associates)

2. **Wilbur Hall**
   Completed 1956 (Spencer and Ambrose)

3. **Escondido Village**
   Completed 1959 (Wurster, Bernardi and Emmons); additions 1964 and 1966 (Campbell and Wong) and 1968 (N. Abrams)

4. **Bing Nursery School**
   Completed 1966 (Clark, Stromquist, Potter and Ehrlich)

5. **Branner Hall**
   Completed 1924 (Bakewell and Brown)

6. **Toyon Hall**
   Completed 1924 (Bakewell and Brown)

7. **Eating Club Building**
   Completed 1951 (Weihe, Frick and Kruse)

8. **Fire and Police Station**
   Completed 1968 (Rockrise and Watson)

9. **Roscoe Maples Pavilion**
   Completed 1969 (John Carl Warnecke and Associates)

10. **Dorothy and Sidney de Guerre Pools and Courts**
    Completed 1973 (Hawley and Peterson)

11. **Stanford Stadium**
    Completed 1921 (C.B. Wing); additions 1925 and 1927 (C.B. Wing)

12. **Encina Gymnasium**
    Completed 1915 (Bakewell and Brown); addition 1925 (Bakewell and Brown)

13. **Athletics, Physical Education, and Recreation Building**
    Completed 1928 (Bakewell and Brown). Board of Athletic Control (BAC); ROTC

14. **Old Pavilion**
    (formerly Encina Pavilion) Completed 1921 (Bakewell and Brown); remodeled 1978 (Barry Brukoff Interiors). Basketball

15. **Encina Hall**
    Completed 1891 (Shepley, Rutan & Coolidge); 90 rooms added in 1917; center section remodeled 1960 (Weihe, Frick and Kruse); west wing remodeled 1969 (M.T. Pflueger). Men's residence.

16. **Encina Commons**
    Completed 1923 (Bakewell and Brown). Men's dining hall; eating clubs; Navy ROTC; News and Publications Service; Public Events; Operations Research

17. **Crothers Hall**
    Completed 1948 (Spencer and Ambrose); addition 1951 (Spencer and Ambrose)

18. **Crothers Memorial Hall**
    Completed 1955 (Spencer and Ambrose)

19. **Stern Hall**
    Completed 1949 (Spencer and Ambrose)

20. **Crown Quadrangle (Law School)**
    Completed 1975 (Skidmore, Owings and Merrill)
    a. Robert Crown Library
    b. F.I.R. Hall
    c. James Irvine Gallery
    d. Kresge Auditorium

21. **Post Office**
    Completed 1960 (John Carl Warnecke and Associates)

22. **Stanford Bookstore**
    Completed 1960 (John Carl Warnecke and Associates); addition 1978 (John Carl Warnecke and Associates)

23. **Center for Educational Research at Stanford (CERAS)**
    Completed 1973 (Skidmore, Owings and Merrill)

24. **Career Planning and Placement Center**
    Completed 1913 (A.B. Clark); remodeled 1967 (M.T. Pflueger). Bookstore; shoe repair shop; Western Civilization library

25. **J. Henry Meyer Memorial Library**
    Completed 1966 (John Carl Warnecke and Associates)

26. **School of Education**
    (includes Cubberley Auditorium) Completed 1938 (Bakewell and Brown)

27. **Cecil H. Green Library**
    (formerly Main Library) Completed 1919 (Bakewell and Brown); addition 1980 (Helmuth, Obata and Kassabaum)

28. **Nathan Cummings Art Building**
    (includes Annenberg Auditorium) Completed 1969 (John Carl Warnecke and Associates)

29. **Thomas Welton Stanford Art Gallery**
    Completed 1917 (Bakewell and Brown)

30. **Hoover Institution on War, Revolution and Peace**
    a. Hoover Tower. Completed 1941 (Bakewell and Brown)

b. Lou Henry Hoover Building. Completed 1967 (Charles Luckman Associates)

c. Herbert Hoover Memorial Building. Completed 1978 (Sprankle, Lynd, and Sprague; Kump Associates)

31. **Memorial Hall**
(includes Memorial Auditorium and Little Theater) Completed 1937 (Bakewell and Brown)

32. **Graduate School of Business**
(includes Bishop Auditorium) Completed 1966 (M.T. Pflueger)

33. **Old Steam Plant**
Completed ca. 1933 (W.F. Durand). Steam plant; power plant; ROTC rifle range

34. **Galvez House**
Completed 1936 (Pole Ford Thomson). Janitors' residence

35. **Terman Engineering Laboratory**
Completed 1902 (Shepley, Rutan & Coolidge; modified by Charles E. Hodges); remodeled 1962 (Edward Page). Electrical Engineering

36. **Havas Engineering Building**
Completed ca. 1893 (Charles E. Hodges); remodeled 1962 (Edward Page). Power house and boiler house; Hydraulics; Materials Laboratory

37. **Civil Engineering**
(formerly Durand Laboratory) Completed ca. 1902 (Charles E. Hodges); remodeled 1962 (Edward Page). Engine house; machine shop; ROTC; Electronics; Engineering; Aeronautical Engineering; Industrial Engineering

38. **John Blume Earthquake Center**
Completed 1891 (H.E. Wing); addition 1908 (Charles E. Hodges). Machine shop; pattern shop; Guggenheim Aerodynamics Laboratory; Industrial Engineering

39. **Peterson Laboratory**
Completed 1900 (Charles E. Hodges); remodeled 1949 (Spencer and Ambrose). Workshop; Civil Engineering; Mining and Metallurgy

40. **Stanford University Press**
Completed 1917; additions 1930 (Bakewell and Brown), 1954 (Spencer and Ambrose), and 1962 (Clark and Beuttler)

41. **Storke Student Publications Building**
Completed 1964 (Clark and Beuttler)

42. **News and Publications Service; Public Events**
Completed 1962 (Clark and Beuttler); remodeled 1977 (Sigrid Lorenzen Rupp). Stanford Press bindery

43. **Word Graphics**
Completed 1916 (Charles E. Hodges). Electric substation; electric shop

44. **High Temperature Gasdynamics Laboratory**
Completed 1908 (H.E. Wing); remodeled 1979 (Spencer Associates). Forge and foundry; machine shop; pattern shop

45. **Building 610**
Completed 1918; remodeled 1966 (Keller and Daseking). Corporation Yard (plant services); Police Department

46. **Old Firehouse**
Completed 1902 (Charles E. Hodges); remodeled 1969. Fire Department

47. **Old Union**
Completed 1922 (Bakewell and Brown); remodeled 1932 (Bakewell and Brown) and 1967 (M.T. Pflueger). Stanford Union; men's residence; women's residence

48. **Building 590**
Completed 1915 (Charles T. Whittlesley); remodeled 1979 (Albert Cabellon; Penny Ching-Chou Mills). Stanford Union; Men's Clubhouse; Associated Students; Union Cellar

49. **The Clubhouse**
Completed 1915 (Charles T. Whittlesley). Women's Clubhouse

50. **Music Building**
(includes Dinkelspiel Auditorium) Completed 1957 (M.T. Pflueger/ Spencer and Ambrose)

51. **Tresidder Memorial Union**
Completed 1962 (Spencer, Lee and Busse)

52. **Bowman Alumni House**
Completed 1952 (Clark and Beuttler); additions 1955 (Clark and Beuttler) 1967 (Hervey Parke Clark), and 1979 (Freebairn-Smith and Associates)

53. **Stanford Faculty Club**
Completed 1965 (Edward Page)

54. **Bechtel International Center**
Completed 1919 (John K. Branner); remodeled 1963; addition 1978 (Hawley and Peterson). Zeta Psi fraternity house

55. **Florence Moore Hall**
Completed 1956 (M.T. Pflueger); addition 1976 (M.T. Pflueger Associates)

56. **The Knoll**
Completed 1918 (Louis Christian Mullgardt). Residence of Ray Lyman Wilbur

57. **Lou Henry Hoover House**
Completed 1919 (A.B. Clark and Birge M. Clark). Residence of Herbert and Lou Henry Hoover

58. **Boathouse**
Completed 1939 (Bakewell and Brown)

59. **Roble Hall**
Completed 1918 (George W. Kelham)

60. **Lagunita Court**
Completed 1934 (Bakewell and Brown); addition 1937 (Bakewell and Brown)

61. **Frederick E. Terman Engineering Center**
Completed 1977 (Harry Weese Associates)

62. **Roble Gymnasium**
(formerly Women's Gymnasium) Completed 1931 (Bakewell and Brown)

63. **Ruth Wattis Mitchell Earth Sciences Building**
Completed 1970 (Spencer, Lee and Busse)

64. **William F. Durand Building for Space Engineering and Science**
Completed 1969 (Spencer, Lee and Busse)

65. **Hugh H. Skilling Building**
Completed 1969 (Spencer, Lee and Busse)

66. **Lloyd Noble Petroleum Engineering Building**
Completed 1957 (Spencer and Ambrose)

67. **Henry Salvatori Laboratory of Geophysics**
Completed 1954 (Spencer and Ambrose)

68. **Applied Electronics Laboratory (AEL)**
Completed 1958 (Spencer and Ambrose)

69. **Electronics Research Laboratory (ERL)**
Completed 1951 (Spencer and Ambrose); addition 1956 (Spencer and Ambrose)

70. **Jack A. McCullough Building**
Completed 1965 (Gardner A. Dailey)

71. **Physics Lecture Hall**
Completed 1957 (Gardner A. Dailey)

72. **Russell H. Varian Laboratory of Physics**
Completed 1963 (Gardner A. Dailey)

74. **Sequoia Hall**
(formerly Roble Hall) Completed 1891 (Shepley, Rutan & Coolidge); reduced to one story 1957. Women's residence; men's residence; Applied Mathematics and Statistics Laboratory

73. **High Energy Physics Laboratory**
Completed 1949 (Spencer and Ambrose); additions 1953 and 1956 (Spencer and Ambrose), 1959 (Spencer and Lee), 1968 and 1970 (Spencer, Lee and Busse)

75. **William F. Herrin Hall**
Completed 1967 (M.T. Pflueger)

76. **William F. Herrin Laboratories**
Completed 1968 (M.T. Pflueger)

77. **Old Chemistry Building**
Completed 1903 (Clinton Day); remodeled 1960 (Spencer and Lee)

78. **Stauffer Chemical Engineering Building**
Completed 1966 (Clark, Stromquist, Potter and Ehrlich)

79. **Stauffer Physical Chemistry Building**
Completed 1964 (Clark, Stromquist, Potter and Ehrlich)

80. **Stauffer Organic Chemistry Building**
Completed 1960 (Clark, Stromquist, Potter and Ehrlich)

81. **Organic Chemistry Laboratory**
Completed 1950 (Spencer and Ambrose)

82. **Seeley G. Mudd Chemistry Building**
Completed 1977 (Clark, Stromquist and Sandstrom)

83. **Stanford Museum of Art**
(formerly Leland Stanford Junior Museum) Completed 1891 (Percy and Hamilton)

84. **Stanford Family Mausoleum**
Completed 1889 (Caterson and Clark)

85. **Stanford Barn**
Completed 1888; remodeled 1961 (John S. Bolles, Inc.). and 1972 (Herand der Sarkissian). Stanford estate; winery; dairy; cattle breeders association

86. **Stanford Medical Center**
a. **Stanford University Hospital**
Completed 1959 (Edward Stone); addition 1976 (Caudill, Rowlett, Scott)
b. **Hoover Pavilion** (formerly Palo Alto Hospital) Completed 1931 (Reed and Corlett); addition 1940 (Will G. Corlett); remod-

eled 1964 (Marracini and Patterson)
c. **School of Medicine; Stanford University Clinics**
Completed 1959 (Edward Stone); addition (Grant Building) 1965 (M.T. Pflueger and Associates/ Edward Stone)
d. **Anatomy/Medical Microbiology Building**
Completed ca. 1905 (Charles E. Hodges). Museum; Bacteriology
e. **Sherman Fairchild Science Building**
(includes Sherman Fairchild Auditorium) Completed 1976 (Stone, Marracini and Patterson)
f. **Louis B. Mayer Cancer Biology Research Laboratory**
Completed 1975 (Caudill, Rowlett, Scott); addition 1977 (Caudill, Rowlett, Scott)

87. **Ventura Hall**
(formerly Casa Ventura) Completed 1926 (Bakewell and Brown). Women's residence

88. **Serra House**
Completed 1923 (Birge Clark). Residence of David Starr Jordan; Computer Sciences

89. **Applied Physics Building**
Completed 1958 (Spencer and Lee); addition 1975 (Spencer Associates). Biophysics; Microwave Laboratory Annex

90. **Edward L. Ginzton Laboratory**
(formerly Microwave Laboratory) Completed 1949 (Spencer and Ambrose); remodeled 1954 (Spencer and Ambrose); addition 1956 (Spencer and Ambrose)

91. **Jordan Quad**
Completed 1961-64 (Claude Oakland)

92. **George Forsythe Hall**
Completed 1979 (Hoover Associates)

93. **Red Barn**
Completed 1870. Palo Alto Stock Farm

94. **Golf Course**
Completed 1930 (William P. Bell)

95. **Stanford Linear Accelerator Center**
Completed 1966 (Aetron-Blume-Atkinson; Charles Luckman Associates)

Index

Numbers in Roman lightface refer to the text; numbers in italic refer to photographs; numbers followed by a "c" refer to captions.

Credits

The following photographers, who have more than one credit, are listed by last name only in the photo credits: Bill Apton, Robert Beyers, Charles Comfort, Jack Fields, Don Flaten, Peter Henricks, Leo Holub, Robert Isaacs, Jose Mercado, Peter Ogilvie, Charles Painter, and Tom Tracy.

Other abbreviations used in the photo credits: Archives for Stanford University Archives; Department of Athletics for Department of Athletics, Physical Education, and Recreation; News and Publications for Stanford Office of News and Publications; SLAC for Stanford Linear Accelerator Center.

Half title page, Henricks; **following half title page** (color), Comfort; (black-and-white), Holub; **facing title page,** Tracy; **facing copyright page,** Reprographic Services, Stanford University; **next two pages,** Henricks; **Introduction,** Archives; **2-3,** Archives; **4,** Henricks; **5-7,** Archives; **8** (spike), Painter; (poster), Sacramento City Directory, 1857; (wine), Apton; (portraits), Henricks; **9,** Henricks; **10** (sketch and spur track), Archives; (portrait), Ogilvie; **11-13,** Henricks; **14,** Mercado; **15,** Henricks; **16,** Archives; **17** (plan), Mercado; (field), Painter; **18,** Archives; **19,** Henricks; **20-21,** Holub; **22-23,** Archives; **24** (capital cutters and construction), Archives; (detail at bottom), Henricks; **25-27,** Archives; **28** Mercado; **29-32,** Archives; **33** (Escondité), Archives; (Hoover House), Henricks; (Alvarado Row), Crandall Collection, Hoover Institution; (Hanna-Honeycomb House), Holub; **34-35,** Archives; **36** (church), Archives; (detail), Andy Williams; **37** (Jane Stanford), Archives; (details), Henricks; **38,** Archives; **39,** Archives (Carl Breer); **40-42,** Archives; **43,** Crandall Collection, Hoover Institution; **44,** Henricks; **45,** Painter; **46-48,** Henricks; **49** (Union), Henricks; (fountain), Painter; **50,** Archives; **51,** Henricks; **52,** Archives; **53** (gymnasium), Archives; (stained glass), Henricks; **54-55,** Archives; **56,** Henricks; **57** (first and second bookstores), Archives; (present

bookstore), Henricks; **58,** Archives (Rose Mandelbaum); **59** (graduation), Tracy; (amphitheater, top), Henricks; (amphitheater, lower), Don Ernst; **60-61,** Henricks; **62,** Isaacs; **63,** Holub; **64** (chair), Mercado; (bikers), Henricks; **65,** Henricks; **66,** Painter; **67,** Fields; **68,** Henricks; **69,** Painter; **70,** News and Publications; **71,** Henricks; **72-73,** Painter; **75,** Henricks; **76-77,** Bob Campbell; **78-79,** Henricks; **80** (new chemistry building and current art class), Henricks; (chemistry lab), Holub; (old art class), Archives; **81,** Henricks; **82** (Varians), Varian Associates; (plaque), Mercado; **83,** (drama), Holub; (Bailey), Archives; (Mirrielees), News and Publications; **84** (Schmidt, Bailey, Maccoby), Holub; (Knoll), Henricks; **85** (old chemistry building and Memorial Hall), Henricks; (McCarthy), Painter; (Gibbs), Holub; **86** (symphony), Henricks; (lake), Holub; **86** (Bush), Mercado; (Momaday), Painter; (others), Henricks; **88-89,** Comfort; **90-91,** Henricks; **92,** Tracy; **93** (Krauskopf), Comfort; (field trip), Archives; **94** (Keen), Margo Davis; (minerals), Henricks; **96-99,** Henricks; **100,** Holub; **101-2,** Henricks; **103,** Archives; **104,** Apton; (Marx), Archives; **106,** Henricks; **107,** Archives; **108,** Holub; **109** (Terman), Fields; (class), Apton; (Terman Center), Holub; **110,** News and Publications; **111,** Henricks;

112 (tunnel), Archives; (Design Loft), Apton; **113** (library), Holub; (student in lab), Apton; **114** (Dantzig), Holub; (student in lab), Apton; **115** (Skilling building), Peter C. Allen; (broken umbrella), Holub; **116,** Henricks; **117,** Ferris Miles; **118-19,** Henricks; **120,** Holub; **121** (Business School), Tracy; (Bach), Holub; **122,** Painter; **123** (students), Henricks; (Miller), Tracy; **124-25,** Henricks; **126,** Stanford Law School; **126-27,** Henricks; **128,** Holub; **129** (moot court room), Henricks; (Amsterdam), Stanford Law School; **130** (Kirkwood), Mercado; (others), Henricks; **131,** Isaacs; **132,** Henricks; **133,** Holub; **134** (accelerator), Henricks; (Kaplan), Mercado; **135,** Henricks; **137** (medical school), News and Publications; (Chandler), Stanford Medical Center (Edgar W.D. Holcomb); **138-39,** Henricks; **140** (Kornberg), Holub; (class), Henricks; **141,** Painter; **142-43,** Comfort; **144-45,** Flaten; **146,** Archives; **147,** Flaten; **148,** Hopkins Marine Station; **149** (Abbott), Holub; (Agassiz Laboratory), Flaten; **150,** Isaacs; **151** (Hoover), News and Publications; (medal), Henricks; **152** (books), Henricks; (Lipset), Hoover Institution; **153-54,** Henricks; **155,** Painter; **156,** Henricks; **157,** Holub; **158,** Isaacs; **159,** News and Publications; **160,** Holub; **161** (excavation), Henricks; (details), Holub; **162-63,** SLAC; **164** (tunnel), SLAC; (Paleoparadoxia), News and Publications (original drawing by Charles A. Repenning, U.S. Geological Survey); **165** (PEP), SLAC (Joe Faust); (bubble tracks), SLAC; **166-68,** Henricks; **169,** Archives; **170,** Henricks; **171** (library and Thomas Welton Stanford), Archives; (card catalog), Henricks; **172-73,** Henricks; **174,** Holub; **175** (circulation desk), Henricks; (tea), Holub; **176,** Archives; **177** (Bender Room), Holub; (Steinbeck manuscript), Henricks; **178-79,** Tracy; **180,**

Holub; **181** (commencement), Tracy; (male faculty members), Holub; (female faculty member), Henricks; **182** (Ross letter), Archives; (faculty, top and right), Henricks; (faculty, left), Holub; **183** (professors), Holub; (commencement), Tracy; (Faculty Club), Henricks; **184-85,** Beyers; **186,** Holub; **187** (Encina room), Archives; (Roble room and square dance), Beyers; **188** (calfskin), Ogilvie; (posters), Apton; (makeup artist), Beyers; **189** (hat), Apton; (present band), Beyers; (old band), Archives; (tuba player), Paul Kegley; **190** (women in hats, two fight scenes), Archives; (plug uglies), Ogilvie; (other hats), Apton; **191,** Beyers; **192** (class on lawn), Bob Filman; (poster), Archives; (*Daily* office and three students), Henricks; (student alone), Isaacs; **193** (Pajamarino and fire whistle poster), Archives; (mailbox), Henricks; **194** (boathouse), Archives; (students), Henricks; **195** (lake), Tracy; (bonfire), Holub; **196** (*Chaparral*), Apton; (residences), Henricks; (little professors), Archives; **197,** Painter; **198-200,** Beyers; **201** (Harry Maloney), Department of Athletics; (building), Henricks; (tickets), Apton; **202** (Nevers and Warner and "Vow Boys"), Archives; (current football), Beyers; **203** (current football), Beyers; (all others), Apton; **204** (programs), Apton; (others), Painter; **205** (water poloist and swimmer), Beyers; (others), Archives; **206-7,** Beyers; **208** (Templeton), Archives; (baseball), Painter; (Jordan), Beyers; **209** (class), Jan E. Watson; (others), Henricks; **210-12,** Henricks; **213,** Holub; **214** (pre-earthquake), Archives; (Rodin collection), Henricks; (others), Holub; **215** (gallery and museum), Henricks; **216-17,** Holub; **218,** Henricks; **219,** Painter; **220,** Apton; **221** (Hoover Tower), Holub; **222,** Henricks.

Maps on pages 44 and 74-75 were prepared by Leo Holub. Heraldic insignia on pages 79, 91, 97, 105, 117, 125, and 133 were created in 1967 by Eric Hutchinson, the University's academic secretary.